Perhaps there are graduate students or faculty members who write as much as they think they should but, if so, I haven't met any of them in nearly 40 years being a professor. But I've certainly met many people who manage to write a lot, and all of them employ one or more of the tactics that Silvia describes. Henceforth, no one should be allowed to complain about how little writing they are getting done unless they have read—and applied—the wisdom in this book.

—**Mark R. Leary, PhD,** Garonzik Family Professor of Psychology and Neuroscience, Duke University, Durham, NC

Silvia demystifies the process of writing and deftly debunks common excuses academics make for not getting it done! The message is simple but powerful: When writing becomes a workday habit, you can write a lot *and* find more time for life outside of work.

—**Monica Biernat, PhD,** Distinguished Professor of Psychology, University of Kansas, Lawrence

In this second edition, Silvia helps readers solve the riddle of writing. By using a mixture of science, humor, and compassion, he shows how he has helped thousands of people become productive writers. If you want to stop worrying about writing, this book is required reading.

—**C. Nathan DeWall, PhD,** Professor of Psychology, University of Kentucky, Lexington

Wherever you are on the continuum from bright-eyed and bushy-tailed newbie to grizzly gray-haired veteran on the academic tour, you need to own this book. And don't just own it; read it. Often. I recommend at least quarterly. You'll nod. You'll smile. You'll fire your writing fervour if you follow Silvia's suggestions. And most importantly, you'll write a lot.

—**Lisa F. Smith, EdD,** University of Otago, Otago, New Zealand

This is a well written, funny, and utterly practical hands-on guide on how to not just write more but also write better, more efficiently, and know how to submit and revise articles. I can't imagine a graduate student, young professional, or anyone who struggles with writer's block not needing this book.

—**James C. Kaufman, PhD,** Professor of Educational Psychology, University of Connecticut, Storrs

Second Edition

How to Write a Lot

Second Edition

How to Write a Lot

A Practical Guide to Productive Academic Writing

Paul J. Silvia, PhD

AMERICAN PSYCHOLOGICAL ASSOCIATION
Washington, DC

Published by
American Psychological Association
750 First Street, NE
Washington, DC 20002
www.apa.org

APA Order Department
P.O. Box 92984
Washington, DC 20090-2984
Phone: (800) 374-2721; Direct: (202) 336-5510
Fax: (202) 336-5502; TDD/TTY: (202) 336-6123
Online: http://www.apa.org/pubs/books
E-mail: order@apa.org

In the U.K., Europe, Africa, and the Middle East, copies may be ordered from
Eurospan Group
c/o Turpin Distribution
Pegasus Drive
Stratton Business Park
Biggleswade, Bedfordshire
SG18 8TQ United Kingdom
Phone: +44 (0) 1767 604972
Fax: +44 (0) 1767 601640
Online: https://www.eurospanbookstore.com/apa
E-mail: eurospan@turpin-distribution.com

Typeset in Minion and Goudy by Circle Graphics, Inc., Columbia, MD

Printer: Bookmasters, Ashland, OH
Cover Designer: Naylor Design, Washington, DC

Library of Congress Cataloging-in-Publication Data
Names: Silvia, Paul J., 1976- author.
Title: How to write a lot : a practical guide to productive academic writing /
  by: Paul J. Silvia, PhD.
Description: Second edition. | Washington, DC : American Psychological
  Association, [2019] | Includes bibliographical references.
Identifiers: LCCN 2018015935 (print) | LCCN 2018017004 (ebook) |
  ISBN 9781433829789 (eBook) | ISBN 9781433829734 (Paperback) |
  ISBN 1433829738 (Paperback)
Subjects: LCSH: English language—Rhetoric. | Academic writing. | MESH:
  Writing. | Research.
Classification: LCC PE1408 (ebook) | LCC PE1408 .S48787 2019 (print) |
  DDC 808/.042—dc23
LC record available at https://lccn.loc.gov/2018015935

British Library Cataloguing-in-Publication Data
A CIP record is available from the British Library.

Printed in the United States of America
Second Edition

http://dx.doi.org/10.1037/0000109-000
10 9 8 7 6 5 4 3 2 1

For Beate, Helena, and Jonas

Contents

Preface

Hello, there. I assume that you're reading this book because you're feeling vexed by writing. It's too slow. There's no time for it. Evenings, weekends, holidays, and family time have become "writing time." You write less often than you'd like but ruminate about it more often than you should. Something has to change.

Helping people change, fortunately, is what we do in the meddlesome field of psychology, my intellectual home. If you look at models of change—whether it is quitting alcohol, taking up exercising, or learning to slowly back away from the open box of apple fritters—you see two approaches. One aims to change you as a person—your values, lifestyle, worldview, identity, authentic voice, and inner past—so that the desired change flows naturally from the new, improved self. The "new you," the theory goes, won't even want the fritters. The other approach, in contrast, ignores that stuff and focuses on changing what you *do*. Cultivating the inner nurturing voice of your authentic healthy self can't hurt, but I think it is faster and more practical to say, "Let's talk about the behavior of picking up apple fritters with your hands and smearing them over your face and chest."

This book sees productive writing as a skill people learn. To write more, you needn't adopt a new writing identity, cultivate an authentic scholarly voice, or interrogate your intellectual values. You're welcome to, if that's your scene, but focusing on specific behaviors that you can do today is faster and more practical. The aim is to make writing routine and mundane, so we'll focus on strategies for writing during the normal work week, writing with less stress and guilt, and writing more efficiently. If you have a deep backlog of projects or worry about finding time to write, this book will help. It won't make writing feel like a wondrous pageant of ceaseless joys, but it will help you get more writing done during the week so that you can have a life outside of work.

* * * * *

Over a decade ago, when I wrote the first edition of *How to Write a Lot*, writing was both fun and vexing. Much has changed since then. My wife and I now have two wonderful children. Lia, our Bernese mountain dog and the unofficial mascot of the first edition, has gone to that big bark park in the sky, and household snuffling duties have been taken up by Athena, our affable and fuzzy shelter mutt. And in a jarring twist of fate that has caused me to question everything I thought I knew about myself, we got a cat. But writing is still both fun and vexing—much like cat ownership, I suppose.

People I work with are occasionally asked, "So, does he really do all that stuff? You know, writing schedules and all those things from the book?" It's okay to ask. I still write every weekday with a slow-and-steady writing schedule; I don't write in the evenings, on weekends, or during long stretches of the summer; I keep track of my writing; and I meet with the University of North Carolina at Greensboro Agraphia group, which has held weekly meetings to talk about writing goals for almost 15 years.

This new edition has the same thesis and themes, but I've expanded some sections. Just in case the second edition wasn't as dispiriting as the first, there's a new chapter (Chapter 8) about writing grant and fellowship proposals. And I revised the text throughout to include all of academia. I never expected readers outside of psychology to hear about the book, but desperation about writing is broader than I thought. A few parts of this edition focus on the social sciences (particularly Chapter 6, which is about writing journal articles) but, otherwise, the book now hopes to speak to a broader scholarly audience. If I've learned anything since the first edition, it's that we all share the same writing struggles.

I'm lucky to have colleagues who like to talk about writing and who tolerate interruptions. For the first edition, many people commented on early drafts and provided encouragement for what must have sounded like a weird project. Big thanks go out to Wesley Allan, Janet Boseovski, Peter Delaney, John Dunlosky, Mike

Kane, Tom Kwapil, Scott Lawrence, Mark Leary, Cheryl Logan, Stuart Marcovitch, Lili Sahakyan, Mike Serra, Rick Shull, my dad Raymond Silvia, Jackie White, Beate Winterstein, Ed Wisniewski, and Larry Wrightsman. Lansing Hays and Linda Malnasi McCarter at APA Books deserve thanks for having faith in a quirky book. Linda deserves extra thanks for a decade of texts and calls and emojis. She knows how to put her finger on the worst jokes and the best Ethiopian restaurants.

For this second edition, it's hard to know where to start. So many people have talked with me about writing, shared their tips and woes, and pushed me to sharpen my ideas. I'm fortunate to work at a university with a vibrant intellectual community, and I'm indebted to my friends in other departments for all they have taught me about the many cultures of academic writing. They might be surprised at how much I picked up from them, but they should know by now that we nosy psychologists are always listening. Special thanks go to the writing group members, Anna Craft, Sarah Dorsey, Alyssa Gabbay, Greg Grieve, Brooke Kreitinger, Patrick Lee Lucas, Joanne Murphy, Anne Parsons, Clifford Smyth, and Pauli Tashima. May your footnotes always be at least as interesting as your text. My recent doctoral students—Roger Beaty, Alex Christensen, Katherine Cotter, and Emily Nusbaum—gave feedback on early drafts of these chapters and served as long-suffering subjects in my ongoing experiments in how to teach writing.

Because of the vagaries of summer travel and children's activities, a large chunk of the second edition was written in small-town public libraries. Working on this book next to a shelf labeled "Large Print HORROR" was both apt and inspiring. My thanks to the librarians, patient keepers of the books.

The only thing that a writer's room needs, according to Stephen King (2000), is "a door which you are willing to shut" (p. 155). This book is for Beate, Helena, and Jonas, for coating the door with stickers, hand prints, and drawings of cats.

Second Edition

How to Write a Lot

1

Introduction

How to Write a Lot is about learning how to write up the ideas you're passionate about while still having a life. It isn't about cranking out fluff, dicing big projects into least-publishable-units, or carving notches into your publication bedpost. Most academics would like to write more than they do now, but they'd rather do it in a low-drama way that doesn't cannibalize their weekends, spring breaks, and family time. This book is for them.

I take a practical, behavior-oriented approach to writing. We won't talk about your feelings, pry into your insecurities, consider your writerly identities or philosophies, or problematize your discourse. We won't talk about developing new skills either—you already have the skills needed to write productively, although you'll improve with practice. And we won't talk about unleashing your inner anything: put your "inner writer" back on its leash and give it a chew toy.

Instead, we'll talk about your outer writer. Writing productively is about actions that you aren't doing but could easily do: making a writing schedule, setting clear goals, keeping track of your work, rewarding yourself, and building good habits. Productive writers don't have special gifts or special traits—they just write more regularly and use their writing time more efficiently. Changing your behavior won't necessarily make writing fun, but it will make it faster and less oppressive.

WRITING IS HARD

Research is good, clean, nerdy fun. Whether your research involves scanning brains, crunching numbers, translating letters, or visiting archives that just happen to be located in glamorous European cities, you're having fun. But writing about research isn't fun; writing is frustrating, complicated, and un-fun. "If you find that writing is hard," wrote William Zinsser (2006), "it's because it *is* hard" (p. 9). How the mind composes text is an eerie and awe-inspiring mystery. We don't know how the brain transforms a squishy mass of images and feelings and symbols and memories into sentences, but we know that it hurts if you do it too often.

Because thinking of ideas is easier and faster than writing about those ideas, most professors have writing backlogs. Passive-aggressive grad students can always score a hit by innocently asking their advisers, "have any interesting projects you haven't gotten around to writing up yet?" The typical writing backlog will range in size from *startling* to *depressing* to *monstrous*. Academics intend to publish those projects "someday," but "some decade" is more realistic. Because they struggle with writing, professors yearn for 3-day weekends, spring breaks, vacations, and the summer months. But on the Tuesday after a 3-day weekend, people groan and grumble about how little they wrote. In a big department, the first week after summer break is a din of lamentation and self-reproach. This sad cycle of yearning and mourning begins anew as people search for the next big block of time. And people usually find these big blocks on the weekends, evenings, and vacations. Writing thus usurps time that should be spent on important activities, like spending time with friends and family, making lentil soup, or knitting the dog a Santa hat.

And as luck would have it, the standards for writing are higher than ever. Our bosses, who hire and promote us, expect more publications than before. All institutions, from grant-addicted research universities to small liberal arts colleges, want to raise their scholarly profiles. More scholars are sending more papers to more journals. More scientists are submitting more grant proposals that compete for a shrinking pile of money. More first-book writers are sending proposals to a smaller group of publishers willing to publish first books. And more scholars have been hired into precarious non–tenure-track positions that, by swamping them with teaching and anxiety over what the future holds, make writing even harder. It's a tough time to start a career in academics.

THE WAY WE LEARN NOW

Writing is a skill, not a gift. No one is born a great writer, let alone a great academic writer. No kindergarten teacher has ever remarked, "I liked your child's essay, but if I'm honest, I liked her footnotes even better." It takes humans an incredibly long time to learn to write as badly as most of us do. In graduate education, though, we spend little time training people in the craft of academic writing, compared with other professional skills. Teaching is hard and important, so graduate students take courses in teaching, apprentice as teaching assistants, and eventually step into teaching their own courses. Research methods are hard, so grad students study it in the classroom as well as in the field, the laboratory, or the glamorous European archive.

But writing—we don't usually have grad classes for that. In the humanities, you often need to publish a book to get tenure, so you would think that one of the many tenured, book-writing professors in grad school would have offered a class on how to do this—perhaps called "How to Do the One Thing That Determines Whether You Get Fired." In the sciences, you often need to juggle a lot of projects, typically grant proposals and a heap of short articles. But grant and article writing are rarely taught in our classes, so most of us would have benefited from a class called "How to Spend Years

Writing Unfunded Grant Proposals Without Sinking Into a Morass of Despair."

In short, few departments offer the same formal training for writing that they do for teaching and research methods. Instead, we teach grad students how to write via an apprentice approach. This sounds good in theory—one envisions impressionable young scholars soaking up the hard-earned wisdom of their elders—but in practice, it looks like a frazzled professor saying, "Oh, that deadline isn't firm; no one turns in their chapters on time." If we professors judged ourselves with cold, sober honesty, would we conclude that we're good role models? Do we complain about not finding time to write? Do we binge write when deadlines loom? Do we meet those deadlines? When our grad students want feedback on their writing, is our turn-around measured in days, weeks, or harvest seasons?

So this is how the bad habits get passed from generation to generation, as each wave of students gets poor training in writing and then models those bad habits for the next wave. And as academia's training languishes, its expectations for grants, books, and articles ratchet up.

This Book's Approach

Academic writing can become a sordid drama. We feel oppressed by half-done manuscripts, complain about cruel rejections from journals, scramble to submit grant proposals the day before the deadlines, fantasize about the halcyon summer days of writing, and curse the foul start of the semester for stunting our productivity. Academic life is dramatic enough already—we don't need this kind of drama. All these practices are bad. Academic writing should be more routine, boring, and mundane. *How to Write a Lot* views writing as a set of concrete behaviors, such as (a) scheduling time to write; (b) sitting on a chair, bench, stool, ottoman, toilet, or patch of grass during the scheduled time; and (c) slapping your flippers against the keyboard to generate paragraphs. Let everyone else procrastinate, daydream, and complain—spend your time sitting down and flapping your flippers.

While you read this book, remember that writing isn't a race or a game. Write as much or as little as you want. Don't feel that you ought to write more than you want to write, and don't publish fluffy nonsense just for the sake of publishing. Don't mistake people with a lot of publications for people with a lot of good ideas. Our aim is to write up what we're passionate about while still having a life.

In Chapter 2, we'll have a look at our most common reasons for not writing. I will show how to overcome these specious barriers by making a *writing schedule*—the idea that animates our approach to productive writing. Chapter 3 delves into writing schedules and describes some motivational tools for sticking to your fledgling schedule, such as setting good goals, managing many projects at once, and tracking your writing progress. To bolster your new habits, you can start a writing group with some friends. Chapter 4 describes a few flavors of writing groups and offers advice for forming a group that does more than vent and grouse. In Chapter 5, we look at strategies for writing well. Well-written papers and grant proposals stand out from the pack, and we should strive to write as well as we can.

Chapters 6, 7, and 8 apply the principles of writing a lot. Chapter 6 gives a practical, in-the-trenches view of writing articles for peer-reviewed journals. If you work in an IMRAD field—Introduction, Method, Results, and Discussion—this chapter offers advice for crafting strong manuscripts and navigating the shoals of peer review. In Chapter 7, we turn to writing books. Whether you are wading through your first book or thinking you might want to write one someday, this chapter considers some common questions and dilemmas. And in Chapter 8, we explore grant and fellowship proposals—perhaps the grimmest genre of academic writing—and learn how to improve your long-run odds of finding success with fickle funding agencies. Finally, Chapter 9 concludes this brief book with some encouraging words.

2

Specious Barriers to Writing a Lot

Writing is a grim business, much like repairing a sewer or running a mortuary. Although I've never dressed a corpse, I'm sure that it's easier to embalm the dead than to write an article about it. Writing is hard, which is why so many of us do so little of it. When they talk about writing, professors and graduate students usually sound thwarted. They want to tackle their article or get to their book, but some big and stubborn barrier is holding them back.

I call these *specious barriers*: They look like legitimate reasons for not writing at first glance but crumble under critical scrutiny. In this chapter, we'll look askance at the most common barriers to writing a lot and describe simple ways to climb over them.

SPECIOUS BARRIER 1

"I can't find time to write," aka "I would write more if I could just find big blocks of time."

This barrier is the big one, the Ur-barrier from which most writing struggles descend. But as popular as it is, the belief that we can't find time to write is still specious—much like the belief that people use only 10% of their brains. Like most false beliefs, this barrier persists because it's comforting. It's reassuring to believe that circumstances are against us and that we would write more if only our weekly schedule had more big chunks of open time. Our friends around the department understand this barrier because they struggle with writing too. And so we thrash through the copse and thicket of the work week, hoping to stumble out eventually into the open prairie.

Why is this barrier specious? The key is the word *find*. When people endorse this specious barrier, I imagine them roaming through their schedules like naturalists in search of "Time to Write," that most elusive and secretive of creatures. Do we need to "find time to teach?" Nope—we have a teaching schedule, and we don't fail to show up for our classes. If you think that writing time is lurking somewhere, hidden deep within your weekly schedule, you won't write a lot. If you think that you won't be able to write until a big block of time arrives, such as spring break or the summer months, then writing your book will take forever.

Instead of *finding* time to write, *allot* time to write. People who write a lot make a writing schedule and stick to it. Let's take a few moments to think about a writing schedule that would work for you. Ponder your typical work week: are there some hours that are generally free *every week*? If you teach on Tuesdays and Thursdays, maybe Monday and Wednesday mornings are good times to write. If you're free and mentally alert in the afternoons, maybe times later in the day would work well for you. If you have a friend who would like to sit and write with you in a quiet room every Friday from 9:00 a.m. to noon, perhaps the two of you could prove that misery does love company.

Chapter 3 digs into the care and feeding of writing schedules, so we'll have much more to say about picking and fine-tuning a schedule then. For now, think of writing as a class that you teach. Most classes are around 3 to 6 hours each week, so schedule 4 hours for your "writing class" during the normal work week. Four hours doesn't sound like much, but it's plenty—approximately 240 minutes more than most people write in a typical week, in fact. Each person will have a different set of good times for writing, given his or her other commitments. *The key is the habit—the week-in, week-out regularity—not the number of days, the number of hours, or the time of day.* It doesn't matter if you pick one day a week or all five weekdays—just choose regular times, chisel them into the granite of your weekly calendar, and write during those times.

I've followed many schedules over the years. My first writing schedule, based on the fragments I can assemble from my parenthood-induced amnesia, was from 8:00 a.m. to 10:00 a.m., Monday through Friday. I would set my alarm for 8:00 a.m., grouse about the inhumanly early hour, and then write for 2 hours at home. Looking back, I have to snicker at my past self. I felt so hard-core when I woke up at 8:00 a.m., like I should drink raw eggs, rack up a barbell, and get a neck tattoo after wrapping up the day's writing. Having kids put an end to that idyllic writing schedule, so I shifted to writing from 5:00 a.m. to 7:00 a.m. at home every weekday—sticking to that schedule for a few years merits a barbed wire neck tattoo. For the past few years, I write on campus after dropping the kids off at school, roughly from 7:50 a.m. to 9:30 a.m.

Instead of scheduled writing, most academics use a stressful and inefficient strategy called *binge writing* (Kellogg, 1994). The drama of binge writing has three acts. First, people spend at least a month or two intending to write, ruminating about their half-done project, and stewing in guilt and worry. Eventually, anxiety over the looming project goads them into claiming a huge chunk of time—perhaps a whole Saturday or the week of spring break—during which they fling themselves at their neglected project with the cold and steely determination of someone suiting up to investigate an odd smell coming from the crawl space. Finally, after an eyebrow-singeing blaze of typing, they emerge hours later, weary and bedraggled, covered in coffee grounds and printer toner, relieved to have more words on the page, but discouraged at how hard-fought those words were.

And then the binge-writing cycle begins anew—more waiting, more worry, more eyebrow-singeing.

Binge writers spend more time feeling guilty about not writing than schedule-followers spend writing. Writing schedules, aside from fostering much more writing, dampen the drama that surrounds academic writing. When you follow a schedule, you stop worrying about not writing, stop complaining about not finding time to write, and stop indulging in ludicrous fantasies about how much you'll write over the summer. Instead, you write during your allotted times and then forget about it. We have better things to worry about than writing, such as whether we're drinking too much coffee or why the cats have started hoarding knitting needles and steel wool. But we needn't worry about finding time to write: I'll just get back to this book tomorrow at around 7:50 a.m.

People are often surprised by the notion of scheduling. "Is that really the trick?" they ask. "Isn't there another way to write a lot?" There are some options you could consider—irrational hope, cussed stubbornness, or intensive hypnotherapy that transforms you into the kind of person who finds writing fun and easy—but, for most of us, making a writing schedule and sticking to it is our best option. After researching the work habits of successful writers, Ralph Keyes (2003) noted that "the simple fact of sitting down to write day after day is what makes writers productive" (p. 49). If you allot 4 hours a week for writing, you will be astounded at how much you will write in a single semester. In time, you'll find yourself committing unthinkable academic heresies. You'll submit grant proposals early; you'll revise and resubmit manuscripts quickly; and, one day, you'll say something indelicate when your pal in the department says, "This semester is killing me—I can't wait for the summer so I can finally do some writing."

SPECIOUS BARRIER 2

"I need to do some more analyses first," aka, "I need to read a few more articles/books/letters/epigraphs/scrolls."

Like all specious barriers, the idea that "I need to do more prep work first" sounds reasonable. "After all," you might say, "you can't write something without a lot of reading." But there's a line between productivity and procrastination—a deep trench, really, that more than a few assistant professors have fallen into while walking to the library to pick up the last book they need to read before starting to write their own.

Academic culture reinforces this barrier. We respect perfectionism and diligence. We know that scholarship requires freakish amounts of reading, laborious data analysis, and regrettably necessary trips to inconvenient archives in Barcelona and Paris. But binge writers are also binge readers and binge statisticians. The bad habits that keep them from getting down to writing also keep them from doing the *prewriting* (Kellogg, 1994)—the reading, outlining, organizing, brainstorming, planning, and number-crunching necessary for typing words.

It's easy to pull away this creaky crutch—do whatever you need to do during your allotted writing time.

Just as it's easy to put off typing, it's easy to put off the prep work, so stuff it all into the scheduled time. Need to crunch some more stats? Need to read some articles, review page proofs, or read books about writing and publishing? Your writing schedule has the space for all that.

Writing is more than typing words. For me, writing's endpoint is sending an article to a journal, a book to a publisher, or a grant proposal to a funding agency. Any activity that gets me closer to that goal counts as writing. When writing journal articles, for example, I often spend a few consecutive writing periods working on the analyses. Sometimes I spend a whole writing period on ignominious aspects of writing, like reviewing a journal's submission guidelines, making figures and tables, or checking page proofs.

Academic writing has many parts. We will never "find the time" to retrieve and read all of the necessary articles, just as we'll never "find the time" to write a review of those articles. This is another reason why scheduling time to write is the way to write a lot.

SPECIOUS BARRIER 3

"To write a lot, I need a new computer" (see also "fancy productivity software," "a nice office chair," "a better desk," "a home office").

Of all the specious barriers, this is the most desperate. I'm not sure that people really believe this one—unlike the other barriers, this may be a mere excuse. When

I started writing seriously during graduate school, I bought an ancient computer from a fellow student's boyfriend. This computer was prehistoric even by 1996 standards—no mouse, no Windows, just a keyboard, a soothing blue DOS screen, and WordPerfect 5.0. When the computer died, taking some of my files with it to its grave, I bought a laptop that I typed into the ground. Even now, I'm writing this book on a "state-contract special" that is so old that it occasionally scowls and shakes its fist at me from its porch rocker. My laser printer is now old enough to run for a city council seat.

If you find yourself blaming your lack of "productivity tools"—an Orwellian euphemism for "high-tech procrastination devices"—remember the inkwell and typewriter. What would your 1920s scholarly self, with its rakish pocket watch or fetching bob, say if it overheard you pining for some fancy new software or device? And what would you say if you heard your 1920s self and its excuses?

- "Blast it all, someone else has the card catalog drawer I need—I can't possibly work on my book today."
- "Curses, reading that source would require walking across campus, entering the library, and retrieving physical printed matter. The indignity!"
- "I'm waiting for the next generation of typewriters to come out before starting my next book. I hear they'll have a number *1* key so I won't have to press the lowercase *l* key when typing dates. Think of how much faster I'll write!"

Scholars wrote lots of books—big, fascinating, profound, important books—before digital "productivity tools" were invented. Indeed, one wonders if writing was easier for them. They could simply write, happily hunting-and-pecking away without the itchy suspicion that someone, somewhere, just said something on the Internet.

What about chairs and desks and rooms? For nearly a decade I used a metal folding chair as my official writing chair. When the folding chair retired, I replaced it with a more stylish, but equally hard, vintage fiberglass chair. For the curious, Figure 2.1 shows where I wrote this book's first edition. That room had a big, simple desk with my laser printer (in its jejune days) and

FIGURE 2.1. My writing room from long ago.

a coaster for my coffee. Before I splurged on that desk, I had a $10 particleboard folding table, which in a nod to fashion I covered with a $4 tablecloth. I wrote most of a book (Silvia, 2006) and a couple dozen articles sitting on my folding chair in front of that folding table.

The more I write, the worse my writing environs become. I've been working at my university long enough to know where the unloved and deserted rooms are, so I usually do my morning writing in a lab room that resembles a place that scientists hastily abandoned in the opening scene of a disaster movie. Figure 2.2 shows where I wrote most of a recent book (Silvia, 2015) and much of the second edition of this one. Note the hard plastic chair and particleboard table with a stylish fake wood-grain top—I've gone full-circle, I suppose.

Unproductive writers often bemoan the lack of "their own space" to write. Perhaps parenthood has

FIGURE 2.2. A recent writing hovel.

shifted my standards, but any space where stuffed animals are unlikely to hit the back of my head will suffice. In a string of small apartments and houses, I wrote on a small table in the living room, in my bedroom, in the guest bedroom, in the master bedroom, and even (briefly) in a bathroom. I wrote the first edition of this book in the guest bedroom in my old house. But that room was eventually lost to cribs and changing tables, so I set up a lounge chair, lamp, printer, and coffee coaster at the end of a hallway. Even now, I don't have my own space at home to write. But I don't need it—there's always a free bathroom.

"In order to write," wrote Saroyan (1952), all a person needs "is paper and a pencil" (p. 42). In fact, Saroyan might have overstated it. As Fowler (2006) reminded us, "You can write only with your brain" (p. 1). We can't pin the blame on old computers and slow WiFi—only making a schedule and sticking to it will make us productive writers.

SPECIOUS BARRIER 4

"I'm waiting until I feel like it," aka, "I write best when I'm inspired to write."

You usually hear this barrier among writers who really, really don't want to make a writing schedule. "My best work comes when I'm inspired," they say. "It's no use trying to write when I'm not in the mood. I need to *feel* like writing." This barrier is cruel because it is half-true. We all have moments when we feel inspired—we lose sense of time, the sentences tumble out, and what we write, as F. Scott Fitzgerald (1955) eloquently put it, is "good, good, good" (p. 7).

Inspiration is like a slot machine. The problem isn't that inspiration never strikes, it's that inspiration strikes erratically and unpredictably. Flow's fickle quality is what hooks us. That's why so many people wait for inspired moments to hit, puzzled about why the muse is forsaking them and their footnotes.

Inspired moments are precious, but we needn't wait for inspiration to do good work. Robert Boice (1990) gathered a small sample of college professors who struggled with writing, and he randomly assigned them to use different writing strategies (p. 79). People in an *abstinence* condition were forbidden from all non-emergency writing; people in a *spontaneous* condition scheduled 50 writing sessions but wrote only when they felt inspired; and people in a *contingency management* condition scheduled 50 writing sessions and were forced to write during each session. (They had to send a check to a disliked organization if they didn't do their writing. The resulting incoming junk mail would have hurt more than the money.) The outcome variables were the number of pages written per day and the number of creative ideas per day.

Figure 2.3 shows what Boice found. First, people in the contingency management condition wrote *a lot*—they wrote 3.5 times as many pages as people in the spontaneous condition and 16 times as much as those in the abstinence condition. People who wrote "when they felt

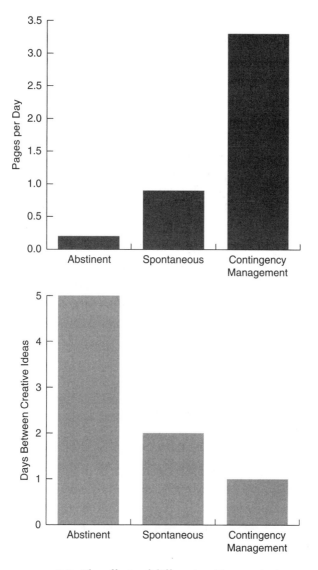

FIGURE 2.3. The effects of different writing strategies on (top) the number of pages written per day and (bottom) the modal number of days between creative writing ideas. Data from Boice (1990).

like it" were barely more productive than people told not to write at all—inspiration is overrated. Second, forcing people to write boosted their creative ideas for writing. The typical number of days between creative ideas was merely 1 day for people who were forced to write; it was 2 days for people in the spontaneous condition and 5 days for people in the abstinence condition. Writing breeds more good ideas for writing.

Another reason not to wait for inspiration is that some kinds of writing are so unpleasant that no one will ever feel like doing them. Who wakes up in the morning with an urge to write about "Specific Aims" and "Consortium/Contractual Arrangements?" Who enjoys writing awkward and self-conscious "yay, me!" personal statements for fellowships? If you have moods where you're gripped by a desire to read the Department of Health and Human Services *Grants.gov Application Guide* SF424 *(R&R)*, you have a bright future. But the rest of us need much more than "feeling like it" to finish a grant or fellowship proposal.

Struggling writers who "wait for inspiration" should get off their high horse and join the unwashed masses of real academic writers. The ancient Greeks assigned muses for poetry, music, and tragedy, but they didn't mention a muse for references and footnotes. Our writing is important, but we don't have fans lurking outside the conference hotel hoping for our autographs on recent issues of the *Journal of Vision Science*. We want our writing to be as good as it can be, but we'll settle for "be" if we can't get "good."

Ralph Keyes (2003) has shown that great novelists and poets—people who we think should wait for inspiration—reject the notion of writing when inspired. The prolific Anthony Trollope (1883/1999) wrote that

> there are those . . . who think that the man who works with his imagination should allow himself to wait till—inspiration moves him. When I have heard such doctrine preached, I have hardly been able to repress my scorn. To me it would not be more absurd if the shoe-maker were to wait for inspiration, or the tallow-chandler for the divine moment of melting. . . . I was once told that the surest aid to the writing of a book was a piece of cobbler's wax on my chair. I certainly believe in the cobbler's wax much more than the inspiration. (p. 121)

How do these great writers write instead? Successful professional writers, regardless of whether they're writing novels, nonfiction, poetry, or drama are prolific because they write regularly—usually daily. As Keyes (2003) put it, "Serious writers *write*, inspired or not. Over time they discover that routine is a better friend to them than inspiration" (p. 49). One might say that they make a schedule and stick to it.

SPECIOUS BARRIER 5

"I should clear the decks before getting down to writing," aka, "I'll write even faster later on if I wrap up all this other stuff first."

This barrier involves ingenious self-deception. We convince ourselves that by avoiding writing, we are actually writing faster. "Sure, I could write a couple pages this week," we say to ourselves, "but if I spend this week clearing the decks of grading and service, then I'll have a clear mind and can write much faster next week." Indeed, a tell-tale sign that spring break is a week away is the sudden flowering of calculus among the humanities professors. "Why write two pages this week and four next week, for an average of three pages per week, when I could write zero this week and 10 next week, for an average of five per week?" they'll say. "It's all about the rates and slopes, people!" If anything could make a Renaissance historian dig into partial derivatives and Laplace approximations, avoiding working on a book is it.

"Clearing the decks" is mental alchemy: We transmute the lead of procrastination into the gold of efficiency. But let's be candid with ourselves. By avoiding writing for a week and throwing ourselves into other tasks, we aren't planning, preparing, or positioning ourselves for a great bout of writing later—we're just procrastinating. And those decks are never going to be clear. We can sweep the jetsam of e-mail and memos and reviews from our humble rowboat, but when our bosses clear the decks of their enormous container ships and luxury yachts, where do you think their rubbish lands? A professor's decks are never clear: there will always be barnacles to scrape, cannons to polish, and scurvy-stricken grad students to free from the brig.

When you use a weekly writing schedule, you stop seeing some weeks as lost causes. The first week of class? Follow your writing schedule. The last week of class? Writing schedule. The week before spring break? Writing schedule. And spring break itself? Maybe you should take spring break off—you've earned it.

CONCLUSION

Humans are immensely creative animals. No other species can come up with such fiendishly compelling excuses for not writing, and only people can make procrastination look productive. Bonobos and orangutans, for example, just sit around and groom each other when they don't want to work on their dissertations, but humans will throw themselves into reading and grading and learning new citation software.

This chapter has debunked some common reasons people give for not writing this week, from searching for time to clearing the decks. We've all indulged in these mental comfort blankets, but it's hard to type when you're wrapped in a blanket. Instead, I developed this book's core idea—academics should schedule time for writing much like we schedule time for teaching and tackle writing's many tasks during that time.

Writing schedules are simple in theory but not always easy in practice. What are good times and places to pick? What project should we tackle first? How can we defend our frail schedules against the work week's many time predators? The next chapter describes some simple tools for turning your fledgling schedule into a fearsome writing habit.

3

The Care and Feeding
of Writing Schedules

Your writing schedule is like is a class that you teach. Just as your other classes meet regularly each week, week-in and week-out, regardless of whether the week is a busy week or an idle week or the semester's first or last week, regardless of whether it is sunny or drizzling, regardless of whether that day's topic is beloved or wretched, your writing class should meet regularly each week, week-in and week-out, so you can patiently teach yourself what you know (Zinsser, 1988). If you like, you can give your writing class an apt course title: perhaps "Anxiety and Panic Disorders," if you're in psychology, "Calamity and Crisis: My Book, 2019–Present," if you're in history, or "Hitting the 'Wall' in 'Qualitative Inquiry,'" if you're in education.

And just as the threshold for canceling your other classes is high—you can stay home if you have a family crisis, an infectious disease, or an embarrassing facial rash shaped like New Zealand—you can miss your writing class only for good reasons. Don't tell your writing course's only student that you canceled that day's class because you "just weren't feeling it" or "had a bunch of e-mail and grading to catch up on." You're both the teacher and the student, so it will probably be your fault if the end-of-semester teaching evaluations are hostile.

But unlike our other classes, our writing-schedule class is invisible: our department heads and deans aren't scheduling weekly times, booking writing rooms, and keeping an eye on things. The motivation to write needs to come from inside, that squishy place where the motivation to exercise, eat right, and spend less time on the Internet are hiding. This chapter thus describes some motivational tips and tools to get your writing schedule off to a good start.

WHEN SHOULD I WRITE?
PICKING GOOD TIMES

In my experience, once people have followed a writing schedule for about a month, they'll be fine, but getting to that point requires some planning. Picking the right days and times is most of the battle. The actual days and times don't matter much, as long as they are *defensible* and *biologically realistic*. A defensible time is like a big castle on a steep hill surrounded by a moat full of ravenous grad students—it won't be invaded by the hordes of service, meetings, and marginalia. For example, 1:00 p.m. to 3:00 p.m. is a convenient time to write but a hard time to defend—everyone wants to hold meetings and classes then. But 8:00 a.m. to 9:30 a.m.? That's an easy time for me to defend. What are your most defensible times? If you don't think you can defend a time slot 90% of the time, the slot is too precarious for your writing schedule.

Defending your writing schedule can require stubbornness and misdirection. People who would never ask you to cancel class to meet with them will see your writing time as expendable. If you say "I'm writing then," they hear, "Oh, she's free then." It's okay to say simply that you "already have a meeting then" and sell it with a knowing eye-roll. Meetings are the above-ground pool professors swim in, so they'll understand. (If you're feeling scurrilous, you can say your meeting is about assessment or accreditation—no administrator would dare interfere with such noble and vaunted work.) One reason why writing groups work, I suspect, is because you really do have a meeting at your writing time, and it's easy and truthful to say, "I have a weekly meeting across campus then." I know some sneaky people who slate their writing times as fake meetings with each other in their department's shared calendar so their colleagues and bosses can't impose meetings then.

Our brains burn brighter at some times of the day, and biologically realistic writing schedules use our high-energy times. In her study of professional writers, Perry (1999) found that around two thirds write in the morning and around a third write in the evening. Not surprisingly, around two thirds of adults are morning people (e.g., Carrier, Monk, Buysse, & Kupfer, 1997), so Perry's writers are respecting their brains. If you pick writing times when your brain is perky, wearing its running shoes and retro headband, you'll write more easily and creatively. But if you pick times when your brain is sleepy or burned out, it will wander away from your footnotes in search of its old sweatpants. You probably know when your best times are, but just ask your brain if you're unsure.

I like writing every weekday, and daily writing has some virtues. Your project stays fresh in your mind, so you'll lose less time finding your files and decoding your unhinged scrawls from the prior writing period. And it's telling, I think, that productive writers typically write daily (Perry, 1999). But writing every weekday isn't always practical, so go with what's realistic. If the vagaries of teaching schedules and family life give you only 1 or 2 days a week, go with that. Many scholars in think tanks or in clinical research, for example, are assigned personal research time, often a full- or half-day once a week. If the boss assigns you Friday morning for writing, then that's your weekly writing schedule. Writing every weekday is nice, but the best writing schedule is the one you can stick to consistently.

Always write during your scheduled time, but don't be dogmatic about writing only within this time. If you want to keep writing once the time is done, or if some time opens up on a non-writing day, go ahead. I call this *windfall writing*. Beware, however, of the temptation to supplant your writing schedule with windfall writing. Don't be the writing version of the person who says, "I don't usually eat apple fritters, but I worked out hard yesterday so it's okay." Writers can't hoard a bumper crop of words to get us through the lean weeks, so we shouldn't reward writing with nonwriting.

WHERE SHOULD I WRITE? PICKING GOOD PLACES

Just as there's no one time that's best for everyone, there's no one best place. Academics write in a freakishly diverse collection of environments (Sword, 2017), from home offices to library carrels, park benches to sandy beaches, coffee shops to public libraries, torch-lit dungeons to abandoned sawmills. If it works, it works. If the gentle scraping and clinking sounds in the abandoned sawmill spark your muse, no one's judging.

But we should be honest with ourselves about the place we pick. Is it really a productive place to write, or is it merely fun, appealing, and convenient? Do we get a lot of writing done there, or is it merely a pleasant place to while away an hour with our laptop open? The human capacity for procrastination is awe-inspiring, and one does wonder if people are slyly avoiding writing by picking loud, distracting places where their pals are likely to interrupt them. Coffee shops, for example, have an idyllic appeal for academic writers. Perhaps you really are productive there. But if you like writing in coffee shops because you can have a great latte while illustrating how a method actor would play the role of "plucky assistant professor with an overdue book manuscript," then you need a new place. Any town large enough for a coffee shop will have a quiet public library.

When you find a nice place, stick to it. Habits come from repetition—doing the same behaviors with the same stuff in the same place at the same times. Our brains settle in for writing faster when they detect that they are in the writing place at the writing time. When your brain sees the abandoned sawmill's bat nests and belt sanders, it will think, "Time to write my book!"

WHAT SHOULD I DO?
SETTING GOALS AND TRACKING PROGRESS

So you have a time and a place: What do you want to write? You might have only one big writing goal, like the dreaded book manuscript you've been avoiding since the last solstice. But you probably have many more—a motley melange of journal articles, invited chapters, book reviews, grant proposals, and conference papers. If so, it's time to take inventory: grab a clipboard, put a pencil behind your ear, and drag all your writing aspirations off the shelves to find any dusty and forgotten ones. Make a big list of everything you'd like to write—your *project goals*—in the next year or two. These goals will range from *definitely* to *fantasy*, but don't judge them just yet.

For example, I keep a list of project goals on a white board at work (and a digital back-up, of course, in case the white board-eating bacteria strike again). The writing projects are divided into *research articles*, *review and theory articles*, and *books*. Some of the projects have been up there long enough to have etched into the melamine, but it helps to have a list so that I know what to tackle next when one project wraps up.

Once you have all your writing goals in one place, it's time to pick one and get writing. The world's oldest productivity advice—after "construct a sundial and Gregorian calendar"—is to break your big, unwieldy goals into tiny, tractable ones. A goal like "turn my dissertation into a book" is too large and lumpy to guide your day-in, day-out work. At the start of your writing period, after shooing the bats away, take a couple moments to think about what you want to accomplish that day.

Day-level goals should be concrete, the kind of goals that you can judge if you meet them. Goals starting with phrases like *work on*, *get started*, or *think about* are too mushy. Consider goals with obvious end-points, like completing a fixed unit of writing. Exhibit 3.1 lists some examples. A clear goal is usually finishing part of your project—like a paragraph, section, or chapter—or finishing a set number of words. Popular with humanities scholars working on books, word goals are wonderful when your project needs some pages. The irrepressible Anthony Trollope, writing with watch at hand, had the concrete goal of 250 words every 15 minutes (Pope-Hennessy, 1971). Those of us who aren't writing romantic political novels might

EXHIBIT 3.1. Daily Writing Goals

The best daily writing goals are concrete. Instead of setting a goal of "get some writing done," consider goals like these for the day's writing period:

- Write at least 200 words.
- Print the first draft I finished yesterday, edit it, and finish the second section.
- Write the first two paragraphs of the Discussion.
- Add missing references and then reconcile the citations and references.
- Read a collaborator's draft, give comments on it, and e-mail it back.
- Make an outline for my next journal article.
- Finish the Specific Aims page.
- Read and take notes on three background articles.
- Read the reviewers' comments on my paper and make a list of things to revise.
- Correct the page proofs and submit them.
- Read some sample grant proposals to get some tips.
- Take an inventory of all my writing projects and list them on my white board.
- Finish the footnotes for Chapter 4.

consider 50 to 200 words an hour. I'm happy if I can get one great sentence.

Nothing helps a writing schedule like tracking your progress. In years past, the notion of monitoring and keeping statistics on your writing would seem immodest and narcissistic. In the more enlightened present, however, people eagerly track pounds shed, steps taken, carbs gobbled, hours slept, and gluten snorted. In a world where people track their bowel movements, rate them on the Bristol Stool Scale, and then share the results online, I suppose tracking how many words you write seems prosaic.

Self-monitoring—keeping tabs on your own behavior—is one of the oldest and best ways of changing behavior (Korotitsch & Nelson-Gray, 1999). It is based on two sound principles of psychology: (a) people aren't paying much attention to what they are doing, and (b) even if they are, they delude themselves about their bad habits. But once people keep records of their daily behaviors for a couple weeks and confront their honest daily records of how much money they frittered away, how often they complained, and how many doughnut holes they gobbled, the stage is set for real change.

Just as people counting steps will take a few more dogged laps around the building so their step counter will pass an arbitrary number, writers tracking their writing can be oddly motivated by the fear of typing a zero into their writing log. Merely tracking a behavior is often enough to change it. People who track their writing focus on different things. Some people track *word goals*, usually with a target of 50 to 250 words per day. Others track *behavior goals*, such as whether they sat down and wrote at all during their scheduled time. And still others track *time goals*, such as writing for a certain number of minutes. A popular time goal involves counting "pomodoros," periods of focused, uninterrupted writing (usually 25 minutes) named after retro tomato timers (Cirillo, 2018). You can pick what works for you: The key is to take an honest look at what you're doing. I usually track whether I sat down and wrote, scored simply as *no* or *yes*, but I find word goals motivating for long projects.

As for how to keep track, I've met people who record their writing progress in everything from fancy statistics programs to online forums to life-hacking apps to wall calendars with smiley-face stickers. There's no best way, but remember what we learned earlier about procrastinating via productivity tools (see Chapter 2)— you don't need a flashy program to monitor and track your writing. Scratching a crude check mark on the sawmill wall wastes less time than scouring the Internet for that perfect app.

Like their dogs and cats, humans will do almost anything for a small reward. When an article goes off to a journal, a book proposal is sent to a publisher, and a grant proposal is hurled into the black hole of probability theory, you can mark the moment with a nice cup of coffee, a good lunch with a friend, or a vintage Hamilton 992B pocket watch. Writing's rewards are delayed—it takes months and months to hear from journal editors and grant panels—so immediate self-rewards will sustain your motivation. But beware the temptation to reward writing with not writing. We don't reward a great day in the classroom by canceling the next class; we don't reward a day of abstaining from smoking by bumming a cigarette; we don't reward diligent, productive writing by blowing off the schedule that got us there.

WHAT'S WORTH WRITING FIRST?
SETTING PRIORITIES

The only thing harder than writing is writing two things at once. Working on one writing project is easy, but juggling many writing projects—some long, some short; some old, some fresh; some important, some barely worth writing—is endlessly vexing. And we rarely get to write only one thing. It's easy to say, "I'm working only on my book this semester," or "I'm not leaving the sawmill until my grant proposal is done," but ever-pesky reality intrudes. While working on the book or grant or touchstone article, many other projects will drift down onto your writing pile: abstracts and papers for conferences, letters-of-intent and proposals for grants and fellowships, short journal articles, book reviews, invitations to revise from an unexpectedly fast journal, and invited book chapters, to name a handful.

Humans don't multitask well. We have big brains and nimble thumbs, but those brains and thumbs find big to-do lists stressful. When people have several pressing goals, you often see what motivation scientists call *behavioral chatter* (Atkinson & Birch, 1970)—people flit from goal to goal, dabbling and switching without making much progress on any particular one. If academic writers don't set some sort of priority rules for managing their tasks, they'll end up like a harried hummingbird with an overdue manuscript.

To avoid chattering, we should pick a way of setting priorities. Exhibit 3.2 lists the most common ones along

EXHIBIT 3.2. Priority Rules for Managing Many
Writing Projects

So you find yourself with a big backlog of projects—what should
you write first?

The most important project: **The project closest to your
scholarly heart—usually a book, big grant proposal, or
touchstone article in a research program—gets done first.**

- *The good*: Your most influential, high-impact scholarship will
  reach the world before your secondary, peripheral work.
- *The bad*: Your most important work might be long-form, taking
  months or years. It is often impossible to stave off competing
  projects for more than 6 months.

Whatever is closest to publication: **The project that is nearest
the door—comments for a collaborator, a revision to resubmit,
or a half-done manuscript—gets done first.**

- *The good*: You won't end up with the menagerie of half-done
  projects that many academics have, and your backlog will
  dwindle as projects get punched out.
- *The bad*: Work that is closest to publication might be your
  least important or interesting work, and ambitious long-form
  projects get deferred.

The oldest project (first in, first out [FIFO]): **The project
you started first gets done first—everything gets knocked out
in order.**

- *The good*: The backlog dwindles quickly as projects get finished.
- *The bad*: The older projects might have grown stale, and
  the newer projects might be fresher and more relevant.
  Your newest ideas are probably your most mature and informed
  ideas. Time-sensitive projects, such as book chapters and
  grants, will suffer.

EXHIBIT 3.2. Priority Rules for Managing Many
Writing Projects *(continued)*

The easiest project: **Whatever project is easiest to finish gets
tackled first.**

- *The good*: Everyone likes a quick win, and this approach lets
  you knock things out.
- *The bad*: Your most influential scholarship is rarely the easiest
  to write. Your books, grant proposals, and top-tier articles won't
  get done.

The most appealing project: **Impulsively jump into whatever
feels coolest and inspiring.**

- *The good*: Writing will be fun.
- *The bad*: We can't trust our impulses to point us toward our
  most important and difficult work, so long-range projects
  will suffer. Excitement and appeal can get people started,
  but projects get abandoned midway when the ardor cools.

---

with their virtues and flaws. Managing many projects
is a fiendish optimality problem in which writing's big
variables—if a project is important, urgent, old, fresh,
easy, or fun—tug against each other. Because there's
no global solution that's best in all cases, each rule for
setting priorities in Exhibit 3.2 has its good and bad
sides. I thus have no grand answer to what I see as
academic writing's most intractable problem. The best
we can do is to reflect honestly about why we're working
on a project—did we pick it because it's easy or because
it's important?—and to ask if we're making the most of
that week's precious writing time.

41

Frequently Grumbled Grumblings About Writing Schedules

"I'm Just Not the Scheduling Kind of Person"

When confronted, binge writers often say, "I'm just not the kind of person who's good at making a schedule and sticking to it." This is mostly nonsense. Psychologists know that people use essentialist, "I'm not that kind of" explanations when they don't want to change (Jellison, 1993). People who claim that they're "not the scheduling kind of person" are governed by all sorts of schedules—we teach at the same times, go to recurring meetings at the same times, and get lunch and coffee at the same times. If we looked at our weeks honestly, even the most flighty academic has as much structure and routine as a trusted inmate at a minimum-security prison.

You don't have to be the kind of person who schedules time for ironing dish towels to follow a writing schedule. Such people really do resonate to routines, but following a writing schedule is easy for even the flakiest among us. Most of our weekly structure comes from our environment, which nudges our behavior. If we want to change what we do—like write more regularly—we can arrange our environment to nudge us to do it. Pick some defensible times and write in the same spot during those times for a couple weeks. Eventually, following that writing schedule will be just another of your routines.

"But We're Just All so Different"

You usually hear "but we're all so different—not everything works for everyone" when someone is reluctant to try something new. As a psychology professor, I can assure you that people really are all so different and unique in uniquely different ways. But people are also all the same—such are the contradictions of psychology (Kluckhohn & Murray, 1948). This book isn't trying to change you as a person. You don't need new values, identities, critical models, worldviews, or hairstyles to write more efficiently. You are fine just the way you are. But if you find that writing is slower and more frustrating than it needs to be, consider making a unique writing schedule and writing something different and unique during those times.

"What About Writer's Block? You Can't Control That"

"Hold on," you might say. "So far, this book hasn't said anything about writer's block. Sure, you can make a schedule, set goals, and monitor your progress, but what happens when you get writer's block?" Like glamorous shopping sprees and perfect first dates, writer's block is a charming notion that exists only in movie montages: the afflicted writer who sharpens pencils, refills the coffee mug, and repeatedly types and deletes the same sentence before stomping off in a huffy cloud of despair.

When people tell me they have writer's block, I ask, "What on earth are you trying to write?" Academic writers cannot get writer's block. It is hard to do what we do, but let's be candid—the prose we write is less timeless than deathless. The subtlety of our linear regression analysis will not move readers to tears, although the tediousness of it might. Readers will not photocopy our reference list and pass it out to friends whom they wish to inspire. Novelists and poets are the landscape artists and portrait painters; academic writers are the people with big sprayers who repaint your basement.

Writer's block is a good example of a *dispositional fallacy*: A description of behavior can't also explain the described behavior. Writer's block is nothing more than the behavior of not writing. Saying that you can't write because of writer's block is merely saying that you can't write because you aren't writing. It's trivial. Giving a fancy name to feeling frustrated with your writing makes your frustration seem more grave and complex than it is. The cure for writer's block—if you can cure a specious affliction—is writing. Recall Boice's (1990) experiment described in Chapter 2. In that study, struggling writers wrote more when they simply followed a schedule—that's all it took. They probably didn't enjoy it, and they probably spent much of their scheduled time scowling at a blank page, but they sat down and wrote a couple good paragraphs in between scowls. Struggling writers who waited until they "felt like it," in contrast, wrote almost nothing.

I feel like a participant in Boice's study sometimes. Having tracked my weekday writing for many years,

I think each day's work can be described with three dimensions:

- *Vexation*: some days, writing was fun; other days, it was frustrating.
- *Quality*: some days, I liked what I wrote; other days, I was embarrassed by it.
- *Quantity*: some days, I wrote a lot; other days, I got only a sentence.

These three factors are uncorrelated—I get all possible combinations. I often write a lot of good stuff when writing was painful; I often write a lot of chaff when writing was fun; and I often squeeze out only one perfect sentence during a day when writing was fun or vexing. I suppose you could take one point in the three-dimensional space—a frustrating day when the output is small and bad—and call it "writer's block," but I'm not sure what giving a label to a lone day's experience buys us.

Writer's block isn't a real thing: it's a shorthand label for "sometimes writing is especially hard" that some people elevate to an inscrutable, fickle force. Just as aliens abduct only people who believe in alien abductions, writer's block afflicts only writers who believe in it. Productive writers follow their writing schedule regardless of whether they feel like writing. Some days they don't write much—writing is a grim business, after all—but they're nevertheless sitting and writing, oblivious to the otherworldly halo hovering above their house.

Conclusion

Writing is a class that you teach: a small class with one student who seems bright but sometimes needs a nudge to get her papers in on time. This chapter is like that student's helicopter parent—it considers some motivational tips and tools for sticking to your writing schedule, week-in and week-out. If you find the right times and places, set concrete goals, and track your progress, your writing-schedule class will be a smashing success—so successful, in fact, that other students will want to take it, a topic we turn to next.

4

Starting a Writing Group

Complaining is the birthright of professors everywhere, especially when the topic is writing: how we frittered away spring break on chores and chocolate, how our grant proposal sounds as compelling as a treatise on maritime law, how our dissertation is going so badly that we suspect that it's planning to break up with us. Complaining about writing is usually bad, especially when it invokes the specious barriers described in Chapter 2. But can we harness the proud scholarly tradition of grousing for the sake of good instead of evil? Can we apply our atavistic academic instinct toward collective kvetching to help us write a lot?

This chapter describes how you can create your own writing group. A good writing group will reinforce your writing schedule, make writing feel less solitary, and stave off the darkness of binge writing. These groups come in many flavors, as this chapter shows, so you'll probably find one that sounds tasty.

What Makes a Writing Group Work?

Nothing in life fails quite as flamboyantly as a dysfunctional group. Because they focus on frustrating, long-range goals, writing groups are prone to collapsing into a smoldering heap of coffee grounds and grievances. If your writing group makes you discouraged and embittered, you should leave and start a new one. Staying in a wayward writing group, like hanging out with the "bad crowd" of miscreants and no-good-niks in high school, will stunt your intellectual development.

Most writing groups work fine, plodding along from week to week, and some groups are excellent. What makes a writing group work? My informal experience suggests that a good writing group involves *voluntary association* and the *lack of hierarchy*: It's more anarchism than socialism (Milstein, 2010). Voluntary groups are made of members who want to be there and choose to keep coming back. You shouldn't force people to attend, but coerced attendance is common once you look for it. A mentoring program for new faculty, for example, might start an "optional, but we can't imagine why you wouldn't want to do it" writing group for its impressionable members. A director of graduate training for a department might require all the grad students to take part in a monthly writing retreat. Directors of large research labs might impose a writing group on all the grad students and postdocs.

Founders of obligatory groups have good intentions—they don't want struggling writers to slip through the cracks. But some people have good writing habits and don't need a writing group. Others are lone wolves who would rather type alone, far from the distracting howls of the pack. And still others are struggling binge writers who aren't ready to change. Coerced writing groups, although common, usually end up with the dour culture of a court-ordered 12-step program.

To avoid a hierarchy, consider putting professors and grad students into different groups. Some professors are alarmed to hear this, their egalitarian sensibilities offended, but most grad students know what happens when professors join student groups. The professor will inevitably slip into a teaching role, turning the group into just another seminar or workshop. Grad students often feel intimidated in a faculty group, erroneously thinking that their writing goals are less important. And, of course, it's hard to do hilarious and pointed impressions of your adviser when other professors are around.

If you're a grad student, you probably have a lot of friends facing the same challenges, so why not found a group? Starting a student-only group is a great way for students to stay focused on their long-range projects, lend each other support, and justify buying the bigger box of doughnuts. But you might keep your writing group a secret from your adviser—he or she might want to join.

THREE FLAVORS OF WRITING GROUPS

Goals and Accountability Groups

It is amazing what people will do to fit in with a group. When high-schoolers conform in ways we disapprove of, like smoking behind the gym or applying make-up with the obsessive fastidiousness of a historic preservationist, we call it *peer pressure*. Academics and scholars have matured, of course, so when we conform to group pressure we call it *adhering to best practices, consulting stakeholders,* and *seeking accountability.*

Accountability is all that most people need out of a writing group. Once we have chosen a weekly writing schedule, we need to stick to it. It sounds easy—and for some people it is—but many of us could use a nudge to stick to our schedule. Tracking our writing (see Chapter 3) is a great nudge, but there's no nudge quite like the expectant looks of our peers when they ask, "So, how was your week?" (Nicolaus, 2014).

I have been in a writing group—the University of North Carolina at Greensboro Agraphia Group—that has met most weeks for around 15 years. Writing-group years are like dog years, so a 15-year-old writing group is old enough to attract the attention of historic preservationists. Our group focuses on accountability and goals, the two big motivational forces that keep people on schedule. The system is simple. At each meeting we read off the goals we set the last week, say if we met them, and then set new goals for the coming week. As you might expect from a support group founded by psychologists, it applies some crafty principles of behavior change.

Keep It Simple

Our group has a low barrier to entry: We run open-ended, come-as-you-are meetings for anyone who wants to show up and set some writing goals. Agraphia meets weekly for around 20 minutes, usually at the coffee shop next to campus, occasionally on campus. Each semester, there's a solid core of three or four people who attend nearly every week and a larger group of people who pop in when they can. A few grizzled veterans have been coming for years and years, much like counselors in a rehab center who were once clients. Other members come for a few months, absorb the basic message and habits, and then reintegrate into society. And some people come only once and decide it isn't for them.

Set Good Goals

Our group focuses on setting goals for the next week. Motivation science shows that *proximal goal setting* boosts motivation (Bandura, 1997). These goals are concrete and short-term, like the writing goals described in Chapter 3. When goals are abstract, it is hard to know if you're making good progress; when goals are long-range, it is easy to put them off. Each member sets a concrete goal for the next week, such as making an outline, finishing a section of a manuscript, reading a book, or writing 1,000 words. These are tangible—you'll know if you didn't do it. Academics are highly trained in using words to wiggle out of awkward spots, so the group should keep its members focused on good goals. The group should gently mock goals starting with *think about*, *try to*, or *work on*—not because thinking and trying are bad, but because finishing is better.

Keep Track

Humans are both frail and forgetful, so you can guess what happens if you don't write down everyone's goals. The next week, a certain convenient ignorance descends upon the members—"Did I say 2,000 words? I think it was 1,000, right?" History may be written by the victors, but it's revised by historians who didn't meet their writing goal. We bring the Folder of Goals to each meeting, and each person says what he or she plans to do before the next meeting. We write the goals down and keep the folder in a HIPAA-compliant file cabinet that shows only minor signs of fire damage at the hands of our chagrined members. And at the start of the next meeting, we lay out the past week's goals and say whether we met them. Figure 4.1 shows a sheet of goals.

We prefer keeping paper records in file folders. It might sound quaint, but our group is so old that our earliest records are cuneiform tablets. And we have had many members who studied history, material culture, library science, and (in all seriousness) historic preservation, so paper documents are what they preferred. But you can keep track in other ways, like a blog or social-media group. Just make sure the members can't wiggle out of their goals.

Don't Overthink It

Your group's members won't always meet their goals. We are busy humans in an unpredictable world, and

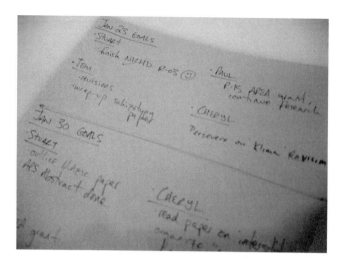

FIGURE 4.1. An example of our agraphia group's goals.

everything takes longer than we expect. It's not a big deal. This isn't a 12-step group that yanks away your chips if you relapse into binge writing. There's no need for a coroner's inquest into what went awry. Just set a new goal—perhaps a smaller, more realistic one—or roll the goal over to the next week. If someone stalls for a few weeks, the group can step in and ask about work habits and writing schedules. But the lines between explanations, excuses, and complaints are fine, so just focus on the future.

The goals-and-accountability theme has many variations, so feel free to vary the group's design. Some groups have one person act as a facilitator; others set an expiration date (e.g., the group will dissolve after a semester or an academic year). Many groups ask members to commit to attending every meeting—usually when they serve nice snacks—and a few discuss books after setting their goals. The peers are the active ingredient. So long as the group creates that adolescent twinge of not fitting in—"Everyone else is going to show up with their writing goals met!"—your accountability group will, shall we say, evoke stakeholder feedback consistent with best practices.

Write-Together Groups

When babies get together on play dates, they do what developmental psychologists call *parallel play*: they sit next to each other but play alone, mostly ignoring each other until another kid tries to snatch Ruffy McWoofers. And what works for 11-month-olds shouting and banging together toy trucks works for assistant professors banging out books on the problematic discourse of transportation. All you need is a room, some people to sit in it and ignore you, and a spill-proof sippy cup for your coffee.

The "shut up and write" model, for example, involves showing up to a room, giving its occupants a curt and flinty nod, and then writing. Some groups meet for scheduled times; others have a drop-in site that's open all day. Some groups meet online, often with video software that allows the group members to see each other ignoring each other—eerie, perhaps, but not the strangest thing that happens on the Internet. A few groups plan long retreats—a weekend in the woods or a week-long boot camp—as a kind of rehab for writing projects that have hit rock bottom.

If your parallel-play group meets regularly, week-in and week-out, it starts to look like a communal writing schedule. And sharing a schedule really works: the mix of peer pressure, habit, and ritual creates a powerful culture of productive writing. The biggest risk of write-together groups is that the members slip into chatty gossip—not a shocking outcome when you put people who talk for a living into a room to work quietly on something they'd rather avoid. To prevent this, you can plan for ritual social breaks—such as the first 15 minutes or after every 50 minutes—and make sure that I'm not invited.

Feedback Groups

Of the many flavors of writing groups, feedback groups are the bitterest. These groups are a TV trope: An aspiring novelist joins a weekly "writing group" that spends each meeting critiquing one member's work, and each member gets a turn in the passive-aggressive spotlight. Humans are too frail for such a system. I've visited with several feedback groups in various stages of collapse, and it's easy to see the design flaws while tip-toeing through the wreckage.

Because only one member is "up" each meeting, that person will spend the prior week binge writing while the other members coast. Unless everyone has similar scholarly interests, few members will have useful feedback on your chapter about colonial imagery in Portuguese admiralty law. And inevitably the system fractures when someone fails to get the pages to the group on time—there's nothing for the group to discuss except the dawning realization that the members are spending hours each week critiquing someone else's work instead of writing their own.

On the bright side, these groups are life-changing when they work smoothly. The members churn out the pages, get insightful peer feedback, find inspiration in each other's writing, and mature intellectually together. A good feedback group is a precious thing, something the members should cherish and keep secret from newcomers who might break the spell. But good feedback groups are rare, and I'd discourage you from starting one. A feedback group larger than a trio of friends usually ends in hurt feelings and restraining orders.

Because this sort of group is popular on TV—it does indeed lend itself to drama—feedback groups are the first model many people try. But most of us don't need our peers for month-in, month-out feedback on manuscripts. If we do, perhaps there's a person—an adviser or colleague—who might help. What we all need is some time (a weekly writing schedule), a place (any location not currently pelted with hail or afflicted by locusts), and a nudge (willpower for some, peer pressure for others). That's what the other flavors of writing groups provide.

Conclusion

F. Scott Fitzgerald (1945) once quipped that "the test of a first-rate intelligence is the ability to hold two opposed ideas in mind at the same time, and still retain the ability to function" (p. 69). Finding myself becoming more contradictory in my thinking as I grow older, I like this idea—probably because it implies that I'm growing wiser when I'm really slipping into the addlepated confusion of parenthood. This chapter considered the two contradictions of academic writing groups: *misery loves company* and *hell is other people*. Bringing struggling writers together creates opportunities for growth, peer mentorship, and the occasional free doughnut. Yet people are wary of joining writing groups for good reasons. Putting embittered writers in a room to coruminate about their stalled projects and thwarted ambitions sometimes makes everyone feel worse, even when someone brings doughnuts. We considered a few flavors of writing groups—goals groups, write-together groups, and feedback groups. Feel free to pick one that appeals to you, and mix and match parts that might work (such as a write-together group that also sets goals).

If you're sitting in the room with your writing group and need to distract yourself from the open box of apple fritters, why not immerse yourself in English usage and style? It will make both your biological and textual corpus sleeker, as the next chapter shows.

5

A Brief Foray Into Style

All written work has a sound—the sound of the page—and I occasionally wonder how to describe the sound of the typical scholarly journal article. A hot air balloon slowly deflating? A shopping cart clattering on a cobblestone street? A hippopotamus falling from a great height? When we talk about our ideas, we sound enthusiastic, lively, and interesting. But when we write about our ideas, something goes awry from the brain to the page—some dark alchemy transforms our glittering ideas into dull, leaden words.

This book is about writing a lot, not about writing well, but we could all be better writers. Improving as a writer takes some time—at least a few months of reading books about style, practicing their advice, and staying vigilant for falling hippos—so this chapter offers a handful of tips to get you started.

Diagnosing the Problem

I like to poke fun at scholarly prose, but there is some wonderful writing out there. All fields have marvelous writers who can inspire us when editing our own text feels like scraping gum from a sidewalk. But when scholarly writing goes awry, it does so spectacularly. To call out any particular writer or field of scholarship would be graceless, but you know bad writing. You have seen it with your own narrowed eyes. Some writing is so dense that sinkholes form beneath it, so malformed that schoolchildren press their faces against the classroom windows to catch a glimpse, so blighted that the page has more pockmarks than punctuation marks.

Ignorance is one reason why our pages sound so stodgy. Few of us were taught writing skills in graduate school. There's always time in the teaching schedule for an obscure seminar on a professor's pet topic, yet there's rarely room for a seminar on writing. And few of our role models in grad school were, shall we say, keen stylists. Vanity is another reason. Academic writers want to sound smart. "If the water is dark," goes a German aphorism, "the lake must be deep." So instead of using good words like *smart*, we choose *sophisticated* or *erudite*. Perhaps I should have said, "Bodies of water characterized by minimal transparency are likely to possess significantly high values on the depth dimension $(p = .032)$."

If ignorance and vanity are the cause, then we know what to do. Overcoming ignorance is easy.

Writers, it turns out, like to write books about writing, probably as a crafty way of avoiding working on some other book. You'll find dozens of good books—just buy one, read it, and repeat at least once a year. *On Writing Well* (Zinsser, 2006), *Sin and Syntax* (Hale, 2013), and *The Practical Stylist* (Baker, 1969) are good places to start. As for overcoming vanity, we needn't abase ourselves as mere worms in the soil of academia to cultivate a more natural and earthy sound. The goal is to develop a versatile voice. Just as good musicians have a broad repertoire and good chefs have more than one signature dish, good writers can write in many voices. Once we can control the sound of our page, be it stuffy or silly, stern or encouraging, dull or fun, we can adapt our style to the audience and occasion at hand.

THE LOW-HANGING FRUIT OF STYLE

Choose Good Words

Writing begins and ends with words, so we should pick good ones. The English language has a lot of words, and many of them are short, expressive, and familiar— make friends with these words. Avoid trendy phrases that sound intellectual, especially ones that make you sound like a college professor. Our lives would be better if we "thought critically" instead of "refracted discourse through critical lenses," if we could "talk more often" instead of "chisel out of our silos." If you're in a silo with a chisel, I'm not sure we should meet face-to-face. Speaking of meeting, people don't "write to say hi" or "introduce themselves" anymore—they "reach out," ideally after using hand sanitizer.

Besides improving your writing, good words show respect for your many readers who learned English as a second, third, or fourth language. Foreign scholars often read articles with a dual-language dictionary at hand. They usually blame themselves for misunderstanding our writing, but we're to blame for leaving them behind.

"But what about technical terms?" you might ask. "How can I write a paper about stimulus onset asynchrony without saying 'stimulus onset asynchrony'?" Fields of scholarship coin words and phrases when they need them—these technical terms do useful work and are easy enough to understand if defined and described with normal words. We should keep our good scholarly words and exclude the bad ones that infiltrate academic writing from business, politics, and warfare (Smith, 2001). We don't need verbs like *to incentivize* or *to target*, and only window washers need adjectives like *transparent*. If fields of scholarship are trapped in *silos*—or worse, *get siloed*—does that mean that sociology and geography are piles of grain and wood chips?

For coherence, use technical terms consistently. Varying terms for technical concepts will confuse your readers:

- *Before*: People high in neuroticism responded slower than people low in the tendency to experience aversive affective states.

- *After*: People high in neuroticism responded slower than people low in neuroticism.

Some technical terms are terrible, so we shouldn't mindlessly copy the words we see in scholarly journals. Psychology, my intellectual home, could do better. Developmental psychologists, content with neither *path* nor *way*, describe developmental *pathways*; when dressed in formal wear, these pathways are *trajectories*. Linguists might *clarify* what *disambiguate* means. Health scientists have clients who *present with* symptoms, presumably like depressed butlers carrying platters of "negative moods" and "poor sleep." Emotion researchers, fearing their readers' ignorance of the meaning of *appraisal*, speak of *cognitive appraisals*, *subjective appraisals*, and—in case someone missed it—*subjective cognitive appraisals*. Psychologists with interdisciplinary interests propose *biosocial* models, *psychosocial* models, *psychobiological* models, and even *biopsychosocial* models; a recent *biopsychosocialspiritual* model surpasses parochial models that are merely biopsychosocial.

We all indulge in bad words, although we usually call them *deficient* or *suboptimal* instead of *bad*. Consider our love for writing about *the existing literature*. Is there a nonexistent, phantasmagoric literature that the grad students should be reading? To most of us, our academic journals are frighteningly real. *Extant literature* is a white-collar version of the same crime. When we write about *a disconnect* between two things, we've become disconnected from our dictionaries, where we'll find good words like *difference, distinction, separation,* and *gap*. And some individuals, when writing individual papers on various individual topics, refer to *a person* as *an individual* and to *people* as *individuals*. *Individuals* is a dreary, multisyllabic word that means, "my grad school adviser didn't smile much." No one says *individual* and *individuals* in everyday life: "Hey, let's meet up with some individuals at the beach and do some individuals-watching." There's nothing shameful about *person* and *people*. We won't mention *persons*, which will remain the property of small-town sheriffs on the hunt for "a person or persons unknown."

Abbreviations and acronyms are often bad words. I've seen writers abbreviate short, familiar words like *anxiety* (ANX) and *depression* (DEP), add acronyms for simple phrases like *anxious arousal* (ANXAR) and *anhedonic depression* (ANDEP), and then dig into the differences between ANX, ANDEP, DEP, and ANXAR. Use abbreviations and acronyms only when they are easier to understand than the tortuous phrases they represent. Some writers believe that they're reducing redundancy by replacing common phrases with abbreviations, but readers find rereading abbreviations more tedious than rereading real words.

Avoid most uses of *very, quite, basically, actually, virtually, extremely, remarkably, completely, at all,* and so forth. Basically, these quite useless words add virtually nothing at all; like weeds, they'll in fact actually smother your sentences completely. In *Junk English*, Smith (2001) called these words *parasitic intensifiers:*

Formerly strong words are being reduced to lightweights that need to be bulked up with intensifiers to regain their punch. To *offer insight* or to *oppose a position* now sound tepid unless the insight is *valuable* and the opposition *diametrical*. The intensifier drains the vigor from its host. (p. 98)

If you took to heart Strunk and White's (2000) command to "omit needless words" (p. 23) but can't tell which words are needless, parasitic intensifiers are basically begging to be totally omitted.

Write Strong Sentences

Now that we're self-conscious about our words—"did I write *individuals* in my last article?"—it's time to turn to sentences. "All this time you have been writing sentences," wrote Baker (1969), "as naturally as breathing, and perhaps with as little variation" (p. 27). By overusing a single type of sentence, we sound like we're speaking in a discursive drone. English has a few types of sentences (Baker, 1969; Hale, 2013). *Simple sentences* have only one subject–predicate pair. We all like simple sentences. *Compound sentences* have two clauses, and each clause can stand alone. Sometimes a coordinating conjunction (e.g., *and* or *but*) connects the independent clauses; sometimes a semicolon does the trick. Unlike simple and compound sentences, *complex sentences* contain dependent and independent clauses. Complex sentences, if written well, give your writing a crisp, controlled tone.

Parallelism—similarity in form and structure—is the skeleton of technical writing. Experienced writers use parallel sentences to describe relationships; beginning writers avoid them because they think that parallel structures are repetitive. Instead, they skew their sentences by shuffling their terms and sentence types:

- *Before*: People in the dual-task condition monitored a series of beeps while reading a list of words. Some other participants in a different group read only a list of words without listening for sounds ("control condition").
- *After*: People in the dual-task condition monitored a series of beeps while reading a list of words; people in the control condition read only a list of words.

Some parallel sentences use a *criterion–variant structure*—they describe what is shared and then describe the variations.

- *Better*: Everyone read a list of words. People in the dual-task condition monitored a series of beeps while reading the words, and people in the control condition only read the words.

Many writers are estranged from the semicolon, a good but neglected friend to writers of parallel sentences. Like their dislike of jocks and the yearbook club, many writers' distrust of semicolons is a prejudice from high school. Work through this—you need semicolons. Semicolons must connect independent clauses;

each part of the sentence must be able to stand alone. Unlike a period, a semicolon implies a close connection between the clauses. Unlike a comma followed by *and*, a semicolon implies a sense of balance, of equally weighing one and the other. Semicolons are thus ideal for coordinating two parallel sentences:

- *Before*: At Time 1, people read the words. At Time 2, they tried to remember as many words as possible.
- *After*: At Time 1, people read the words; at Time 2, they tried to remember as many words as possible.
- *Before*: People in the reading condition read the words, and people in the listening condition heard a recording of the words.
- *After*: People in the reading condition read the words; people in the listening condition heard a recording of the words.

While you're rebuilding your relationship with the semicolon, make a new friend—the dash. Technically called *em dashes*—they're the width of a capital M— dashes enable crisp, striking sentences. Dashes have two common uses (Gordon, 2003). First, a single dash can connect a clause or phrase to the end of sentence. You've read a lot of these in this chapter:

- Work through this—you need semicolons.
- While you're rebuilding your relationship with the semicolon, make a new friend—the dash.

Second, two dashes can enclose a parenthetical expression. You've read these, too:

- Now that we're self-conscious about our words—"did I write *individuals* in my last article?"—it's time to turn to sentences.
- Technically called *em dashes*—they're the width of a capital M—dashes enable crisp, striking sentences.

Try using dashes for your next Participants and Design section:

- *Okay*: Forty-two adults participated in the experiment. There were 12 women and 30 men.
- *Better*: Forty-two adults—12 women and 30 men—participated in the experiment.

The em dash has a lesser known cousin, the *en dash*. The width of a capital N, the en dash coordinates two concepts. It's a clean way of expressing *between*. Few writers use en dashes properly; they use hyphens instead, often with funny results. Developmental psychologists interested in *parent-child behavior* probably don't mean that parents act like babies sometimes—they mean *parent–child*, a shorthand for "behavior between parents and children." You should know the difference between a *teacher–parent conference* (en dash) and a *teacher-parent conference* (hyphen). A researcher on my campus posted flyers for an "infant-parent interaction study." Forget teen pregnancy—let's stop infant pregnancy. Now is a good time to thank the valiant copyeditors who have silently corrected the en dash errors in our published work.

We can strengthen our sentences by experimenting with appositional phrases. Because the positions of phrases in a sentence imply relationships, we can chop words that connect and coordinate parts of the sentence.

- *Before*: *Counterfactual thoughts*, which are defined as thoughts about events that did not occur, illustrate the intersection of cognition and emotion.

- *After*: *Counterfactual thoughts*, defined as thoughts about events that did not occur, illustrate the intersection of cognition and emotion.

- *Better*: *Counterfactual thoughts*—thoughts about events that did not occur—illustrate the intersection of cognition and emotion.

- *Before*: The study of facial expressions is a popular area within the study of cognition and emotion, and it has settled old conflicts about the structure of emotions.

- *After*: The study of facial expressions, a popular area within the study of cognition and emotion, has settled old conflicts about the structure of emotions.

When you're hunting for opportunities to use ablatives and appositives, *such that* is easy prey. You rarely hear someone say *such that* out loud, but you see it in afflicted writing. Let's envision a world without *such that* and be the change. If your word processor's search function turns up a few cases, you have three options:

delete the clause preceding *such that*, replace *such that* with a colon or dash, or write a tighter sentence.

- *Before*: We created two conditions such that people in one condition were told to be accurate and people in another condition were told to be fast.
- *After*: People in one condition were told to be accurate; people in another condition were told to be fast. (Dropped the preceding clause, used a semicolon to create parallel clauses.)
- *After*: We created two conditions: People in one condition were told to be accurate, and people in another condition were told to be fast. (Replaced *such that* with a colon.)
- *Before*: People were assigned to groups such that the assignment process was random.
- *After*: People were randomly assigned to groups. (Wrote a tighter sentence.)

Avoid Passive, Limp, and Wordy Phrases

All books about writing urge people to write in the active voice. People think actively and speak actively, so active writing captures the compelling sound of everyday language. Passive writing, by hiding the sentence's agent, strikes people as vague and evasive. Writers who want to sound smart drift toward the passive voice; they like its impersonal sound and its stereotypical association with scholarly writing. Passive writing is easy to fix. Read your writing and circle each appearance of *to be*. Can you think of a better verb?

Nearly all verbs imply being, so you can usually replace *to be* with dynamic verbs. Change at least one third of your original uses of *to be*. With vigilance and practice, you'll write fewer passive sentences.

To revive enervated sentences, negate with verbs instead of with *not*. People often miss *not* when reading and thus misunderstand your sentence. This trick shortens your sentences and expresses your points vividly.

- *Before*: People often do not see *not* when reading and thus do not understand your sentence.
- *After*: People often miss *not* when reading and thus misunderstand your sentence.

Some common phrases are aggressively passive. In any journal, you'll find researchers "ivving it up": their results are indicative of significance, the theory is reflective of its historical context, the data are supportive of the hypothesis. This is passive writing at its most flamboyant and unapologetic: the writer chose an awkward, passive form instead of a common, active form. Delete all to *be* _____*ive of* phrases by rewriting the verb:

- *to be indicative of = to indicate*
- *to be reflective of = to reflect*
- *to be supportive of = to support*
- *to be implicative of = to imply*
- *to be suggestive of = to suggest*

I have a memory of reading *is confirmative of*—a false memory, I hope.

Only vigilance will stop wordy phrases from wandering into your sentences. You often see, for example, statements like "attitudes are emotional in nature." If attitudes are emotional in nature, what are they like in captivity? Will they reproduce more readily than captive pandas? Likewise, let's avoid *in a _____ manner*. Use adverbs—"people responded *rapidly*" instead of "people responded *in a rapid manner*"—to avoid a tragedy of manners. Even active sentences can be limp and lifeless. Scientists often start a sentence with "Research shows that . . . ," "Many new findings suggest that . . . ," or "A monstrous amount of research conclusively proves that . . ." These phrases add little to our meaning, and a couple citations at the end of the sentence will show that research bolsters your point. You'll need these phrases occasionally, but avoid them when possible.

Writers hobble strong sentences by starting with lumpy phrases like "However . . . ," "For instance . . . ," and "For example . . ." Move *however* into the first joint of the sentence:

- *Before*: However, recent findings challenge dual-process theories of persuasion.
- *After*: Recent findings, however, challenge dual-process theories of persuasion.

Relocate *for example* and *for instance* when it sounds good, but keep *but* and *yet* at the start of the sentence. As an aside, remember that a poorly punctuated *however* can turn a compound sentence into a glorious run-on.

- *Before*: High self-efficacy enhances motivation for challenging tasks, however it reduces motivation if people perceive the task as easy.
- *After*: High self-efficacy enhances motivation for challenging tasks; however, it reduces motivation if people perceive the task as easy.

Don't stew in shame and self-recrimination when you write passive sentences. Scholarly writing addresses impersonal agents—concepts, theories, constructs, relationships. We often have weak agents, such as *past research*, *behavioral therapy*, or *the cognitive approach to anxiety disorders*. When readers can't easily form a mental image of the subject and its action—a theory making predictions, a concept correlating with another concept, a tradition influencing modern research— active sentences lose their punch. There is a place for sentences that start with *There is* and *There are*. Sometimes the passive voice is best.

WRITE FIRST, REVISE LATER

Generating text and revising text are distinct parts of writing—don't do both at once. The goal of text generation is to throw confused, wide-eyed words on a page; the goal of text revision is to scrub the words clean so that they sound nice and can go out in public. Some writers try to write a pristine first draft, one free of flaws and infelicities, but I think the quest for the perfect first draft is misguided. Writing this way is too stressful. These writers compose a sentence; worry about it for

5 minutes; delete it; write it again; change a few words; and then, exasperated, move on to the next sentence. Perfectionism is paralyzing.

We should master the principles of style, but we needn't obsess about them when we sit down to write. Revising while generating text is like drinking decaf in the morning: a noble idea, wrong time. It's okay if your first drafts sound like they were hastily translated from Icelandic. Writing is part creation and part criticism, part id and part superego: let the id unleash a discursive screed, and then let the superego, with its red pens and eye rolls, have its turn.

CONCLUSION

This chapter sought to make you self-conscious about your writing. Many individuals display inaccurate self-assessments of their deficient writing skill levels—or to borrow Zinsser's (2006) crisp sentence: "Few people realize how badly they write" (p. 17). Strong, clear writing will make your work stand out from the dry and obtuse crowd. Read some good books about style, practice the principles of good writing when you generate and revise text, and avoid writing the word *individuals*.

Now that you have a sturdy schedule and a sleek sense of style, it's time to chip through your backlog of research articles. What makes articles appealing to readers and reviewers? The next chapter considers some tips from the muddy trenches of peer-reviewed journals.

6

Writing Journal Articles

Scholarly journals are like the mean jocks and aloof rich girls in every 1980s high-school movie: They reject all but the beautiful and persistent. A manuscript must be appealing and shiny to catch the eye of the cool crowd that picks which papers get published. And it must be determined and resilient to squeeze its way past the many dozens of other suitors competing for the editor's affections. So how do we write manuscripts that are both pretty and gritty?

After a couple decades in the muddy trenches of scholarly journals—as an author, reviewer, and editor—I've learned that the process of peer review is largely reasonable, predictable, rational, and fair—not entirely, and not overwhelmingly, but largely. And if we understand how any reasonably predictable system works, we can nudge it to do what we want.

This chapter talks about beauty and persistence, the two things writers can control to have better odds at the journals. For the first, beauty, we'll describe how to write better papers. As shocking as it sounds, better papers have better odds. For the second, persistence, we'll describe how to interact with journals, which strike beginners as cold and fickle. We'll focus on IMRAD articles—the Introduction, Method, Results, and Discussion structure common in the social and health sciences—but the general advice applies to everyone on the outside looking in.

PICK YOUR AUDIENCE FIRST

Obviously, we should write our articles with the assumption that people will read them. But who? Nearly all scholarly work can be crafted to appeal to different audiences, so you need to pick one before writing. Our articles aren't so different from rock songs. A good song can be arranged to make the hipsters bob their heads in a small basement club, rearranged to appeal to selfie-snapping teens in a huge arena, and rearranged yet again when the lead singer embarks on an emotionally overwrought acoustic coffeehouse tour after getting out of rehab.

Articles have themes and hooks and arcs that can be arranged to appeal to different crowds. Instead of "writing an article," we should always "write an article for . . ." There's no one-size-fits-all structure, no plain-vanilla format, for a scholarly field's articles. We might teach a plain-vanilla format to undergraduates in research methods classes, but what works in rehearsal doesn't always make the crowd dance. For example, perhaps you've just wrapped up a study of how adults with depression talk to their children about goals and values. This work could go to journals in clinical psychology, developmental psychology, family studies, motivation and emotion, or social psychology. Each area would expect to see something different—in length, tone, emphasis, details, and references—so you should pick your audience first.

Choosing your target journal is thus the first step in writing. If you know who you're writing for, you can craft the paper to appeal to them. Most of your vexing writing decisions can be solved by using that journal's published articles as models. How long should the Introduction be? Should you make a table of your sample's demographic statistics? Do you have to have sections devoted to limitations or future directions? Should you post online data and supplemental materials? Should the tone be detached and stuffy or personal and earthy? Do what the articles in that journal typically do.

WRITING AN IMRAD EMPIRICAL ARTICLE

Writing a journal article is like writing a screenplay for a romantic comedy—you need to learn a formula. But instead of meet-cutes and quirky best friends, we have the IMRAD: Introduction, Method, Results, and Discussion.

Outlining and Planning

On my list of maladaptive practices that make writing harder, Not Outlining is pretty high—just above Typing

With Scratchy Wool Mittens, just below Training My Dog to Take Dictation. Outlining is writing, not a prelude to "real writing." Like hypochondriacs, writers who don't outline are convinced that they're afflicted with a mystifying illness—the fake malady of writer's block, in this case (see Chapter 3). After trying to write blindly, they feel frustrated and complain about how hard it is to generate words. "Clear thinking becomes clear writing," said Zinsser (2006, p. 8). We're not doing improv, so let's collect our thoughts before stepping onto the stage.

Your article should always fit within the typical length of published articles in your target journal, but it's better to be on the brief end. Short is good. When you read journal articles, how often do you wish that the authors would keep their momentum going for another eight pages? Some authors are like self-indulgent jam bands who keep riffing on the same themes—yet another secondary finding, another future direction, another arcane implication. Just enough is usually just right.

The Title and Abstract

Most readers who come across your article will see only the title and abstract, so make them count. A good title balances generality and specificity—say what your article is about, but don't be so specific that your article sounds technical and tedious. If tempted to write a trendy, topical, or comical title, think about how it will sound in 10 years. Will future researchers get the joke? Readers in our digital age find our articles with electronic databases, so your abstract should be stuffed with the keywords that you would want found in a database search, even if the abstract's style suffers.

Introduction

Writers fear the Introduction, the hardest section to write, and for good reasons. This section gets the most scrutiny from readers and reviewers, so the article's success hinges on how well we can make our case. For most articles, the time-honored *books-and-bookends* formula (Silvia, 2015, p. 97) will make your Introduction sleek and compelling. This formula divides the Introduction into brief opening and closing sections that flank longer chunks of ideas, much like small bookends holding books upright.

- Your Introduction starts with a brief overview of your work, usually one or two paragraphs long, that sets the stage. This first bookend, often called the "Pre-Introduction" or the "Intro to the Intro," starts with the global issues that animate your work and then funnels into a snapshot of your project. This section usually ends with a sentence that hits the paper's primary purpose, such as a sentence starting with, "In the present research, we examined. . . ." A good Pre-Introduction gives a snapshot of the paper's animating problem.
- After your first bookend, you have your books. When outlining, think of this section as a set of chunks—usually two, three, or four main pieces.

Ultimately, most Introductions have only two or three parts, each marked by a heading. Once you figure out those parts, writing the Introduction is simple. Your first section, for example, might summarize the state of knowledge about your problem; your second section might introduce a complicating issue (why does it happen? how does it work?); and your third section might describe how the complicating issue can be addressed. Likewise, your first section might describe one theory, your second might describe a competing one, and your third might explain how to evaluate which one is better. The details, of course, will vary, but cleaving your ideas into two to four chunks is a good outlining tactic.

■ Finally, you conclude your Introduction with the other bookend, which starts with a heading called something like *The Present Research*. So far, you have given an overview of your problem (your Pre-Introduction) and developed your reasoning for the research (your two to four books). By now, the reader understands your study's context and significance. This final section gives a snapshot of your research and explains how it answers your guiding question—it might take one to four paragraphs, depending on the level of detail. Conclude this section with the heading that begins your Method section (*Method* or *Study 1*).

The books-and-bookends formula is crisp: It introduces the reader to your problem, lays out the theories and research relevant to the problem, and illustrates how your research will solve the problem. It leads both the reader and the writer on a straight path and discourages straying from the main points. You'll find exceptions to this formula—for short reports, a single section with no headings suffices— but the books-and-bookends template works well for most articles.

Method

Method sections are easy, the low-hanging fruit that weak-willed writers pick first when starting a new manuscript. Writing them is even easier if you choose your journal first, because you can use their published articles as models. Method sections aren't glamorous, but they reveal how carefully you conducted your research (Reis, 2000). Like introductions, they follow a formula made up of subsections. The first, *Participants* or *Participants and Design*, describes the size and characteristics of the sample and, for experiments, the experimental design. If your study hinged on equipment, you'll need a subsection called *Apparatus*. A *Measures* subsection is helpful when your research used assessment tools, such as neurocognitive tests, interest inventories, and self-report measures of attitudes.

After these subsections, you have the *Procedure* subsection, the heart of your Method. In this section, describe what you did and said. Reviewers pay close attention to the procedure subsection, and you don't want to look like you're hiding something. Provide a lot of detail about your independent variables and dependent variables. Your rhetorical goal is to connect your procedures with the procedures used in published articles. If your experiment used a manipulation that has been used before, cite representative past experiments, even if the manipulation is well-known. If you invented the manipulation, cite research that used similar manipulations or research that implies that your manipulation is reasonable. Connecting your procedures to past research allays concerns about the validity of what you did.

Reviewers want to know how you measured your dependent variables. If your dependent variables are well established, cite articles that developed or used the scales. For professional tests, cite the test manuals as well as recent articles that used the tests. For self-report scales, list the scale values—for example, 7-point scales can be 1 to 7, 0 to 6, or −3 to +3—along with any labels that anchored the scale (e.g., 1 = *not at all*, 7 = *extremely*). If your dependent measures were physiological or behavioral, briefly describe past research that supports the validity of your measure.

Results

The Results section is where you display and describe your findings. Your statistics should be like paintings in a museum hallway that readers walk through—each major piece gets plenty of space and some handy interpretive text. Order, emphasis, and selectivity are important.

A good Results section will use headings to segregate the dense clusters of findings. Your first heading marks a subsection for the ugly bits (Salovey, 2000). This part, usually called something like "Data Reduction and Analysis Plan," contains essential but tedious analytic facts. They need to be in there somewhere, but concentrating them in one place makes the Results sleeker. This section, for example, is where you would describe how you formed composite scores, evaluated reliability, tested statistical assumptions, and crunched the numbers. Such arcana are best shoveled into this first section, which is the subtle maintenance closet at the start of the hallway.

Next, you'll need a heading for the main findings. The most central findings come first—your primary hypotheses, your primary measures—and decline from there (Salovey, 2000). It's key to know when to stop. Researchers can be easily enchanted by peripheral findings, but we can't describe everything. Just as all museums have heaps of paintings in the basement vault that they could have displayed, you probably have heaps of peripheral findings that you find fascinating but would clutter the walls. Readers get confused, and your Results section loses steam as readers slog through the morass of marginalia. Peripheral findings can be stuffed into footnotes or, better yet, online supplemental information that can be accessed by the few readers who share your enchantment.

When describing your findings, use a *remind-describe-explain* format. At the start of a segment, remind readers of your hypothesis, describe the outcome of the analysis, and then briefly explain what it means. Your Discussion will have the extended recaps and interpretations; here, you have the brief, tasteful sign next to the painting. For example, here's a blunt, context-free segment:

> According to a t-test, the mean depression scores were significantly different between the treatment and wait-list control groups, $t(78) = 3.32$, $p < .001$.

Readers would rather read this, however:

> Did the intervention affect levels of depression? A t-test on BDI scores (see Table 2) revealed that the intervention did significantly affect depression scores, $t(78) = 3.32$, $p < .001$. As our model predicted, people who received short-term social skills training were less depressed than people in the wait-list control condition.

A museum-quality Results section achieves a sleek and spare look by moving as much information as possible to tables and figures. If we're describing an experiment with four cells, for example, no one wants to read dense paragraphs stuffed with means, standard errors, and confidence intervals for each outcome for each condition. But if we make an elegant figure with the means and error bars, a comprehensive table of descriptive statistics, or both of them, our readers are doubly happy. They can see both an easy-to-read paragraph as well as tables and figures that convey much more statistical detail than the paragraph could possibly hold. Your Results section will obviously always contain numbers, but aim for discourse over digits whenever possible.

Discussion

The Discussion steps back and puts your findings in context. The typical one is a drama in three parts.

- Start with a recap, a one- to three-paragraph over-view. After sifting through the piles of nuts and bolts in your Method and Results, your readers want to be reminded of what you're trying to build. Your recap thus goes back to the big issues in the Introduction. Begin with the conceptual issues, funnel toward the hypotheses, and then describe how your results inform the big questions that animate your article. A good recap resembles a long abstract of the Introduction and Results.

- After the recap, build connections with past work by discussing a couple ways in which your work matters. Perhaps your findings have implications for how your readers should think about past theories, methods, practices, or articles. We all see our work as rich with implications, but pick the most interesting and important ones. If you discuss more than three, you'll start to sound like a self-indulgent jam band.

- The third section wraps up any remaining issues. Any quirks or problems in the Results to confront? Any directions for future research? Any practical applications? Any limitations? Most of the topics in this section are optional at some journals but required at others. In some fields, you must always have a section on limitations and a section on future directions; in other fields, some papers have them but others don't. You should consult recent articles in your target journal. If most of the articles don't include these sections, you can omit them for the sake of a sleek Discussion. If you like, you can end with a short concluding paragraph, but it's optional.

About that limitations section: Your under-graduate research-methods instructor told you to end your Discussion with a section on limitations; your thesis committee probably wanted this section, too. Describing limitations is a useful educational exercise, but it's often pointless in an article intended for a professional journal. Most of what pass for limitations are merely directions for future research. Yes, it would have been nice to have a larger sample with a broader range of ages, regions, and cultures; yes, it would have been nice to have even fancier methods and more time points; yes, it's conceivable that a different study that uses different measures with a different sample would find something different. Other limitations are so generic to an area of research that it's irksome to reread the same paragraph of ritual self-flagellation in every article. As always, do what the articles in your target journal do—but if they don't indulge in the ritualistic self-abasement of the generic limitations paragraph, omit it.

References

Although not as glamorous as an Introduction or as brawny as the Results, your References section deserves to be done well. Your references say a lot about how you view your work. Apart from documenting the sources that influenced your ideas, they position you within a field of scholarship. If you're sending your paper to a family studies journal, for example, but rarely cite articles from those journals, you'll look like an interloper who wants an audience without taking the trouble to connect to it.

SUBMITTING YOUR MANUSCRIPT

When is your fledgling manuscript ready to leave the nest? The frazzled and flaky submit their papers too early, thinking, "I'll just send it off now and clean it up later when I resubmit it." The perfectionists, on the other hand, can't bear to stop tweaking and sanding and polishing as they fret about the imagined scowls of reviewers who noticed an errant *their/there* typo. In this case, the perfectionists are probably right. Editors are more likely to invite a revision when the first draft is tight because the author seems like someone who would resubmit a revision without much drama.

Before submitting your pristine manuscript, don't forget to read the journal's instructions to authors. Submission guidelines vary between journals and change over the years, so they are always worth double checking. These days, virtually all journals manage submissions via an online system—everything else seems suspiciously retro. If a journal wants you to mail a hard copy of your paper to the editorial office, be sure to ask where the Pony Express courier should deliver it.

Regardless of how you submit your manuscript, you'll need to write a cover letter to the editor. Most people dash off a boilerplate letter with the standard disclosures and statements; a few write a treatise that summarizes the manuscript and extols its many merits and charms. If your paper's merits and charms aren't self-evident, a long and labored cover letter won't help you—keep it short and simple. Some journals invite you to list a few possible reviewers and to note anyone who shouldn't review it. Don't be shy about suggesting a few people who could give your paper an informed reading, but don't be crass about suggesting your bros and besties from grad school or anyone with a clear conflict of interest. You'll lose credibility with the editors, who have long memories for such shenanigans.

Understanding Reviews and Resubmitting Your Manuscript

What should we do once we submit our paper? Turn to the next one, naturally. We don't reward productive writing by not writing (see Chapter 3), so chip away at your backlog while you wait to hear back from the journal. Experience shows that the editor's action letter will arrive at the most inconvenient time, usually when a grant proposal is due in 2 weeks or you're 85% done with another manuscript.

When the editor's action letter arrives, read it. If you feel the need for some "emotional distance" before reading the reviews, strive instead for "intellectual closeness." Your writing backlog is too vast and obdurate to care about your fragile fears and feelings. Setting aside the reviews for a few days is precious self-indulgence. Read the reviews and make a plan. The editor's decision can take three forms: (a) the manuscript has been accepted; (b) the door is cracked open for a resubmission; or (c) the door is closed, locked, and sealed with crime-scene tape. Acceptance decisions are usually obvious. The editor says the manuscript has been accepted and tells you to expect some forms; sometimes, the editor accepts a manuscript pending minor changes. Although it's rare that the first submission of a manuscript is accepted outright, it happens—one more reason to submit excellent first drafts.

When the door is open, the editor is willing to consider a revised version of your manuscript. This category ranges from encouraging letters that imply likely acceptance to discouraging letters that imply a long slog of revision. Wide-open doors involve easy changes, such as rewriting parts of the text or adding information. Barely open doors involve tedious changes, such as collecting more data and rewriting most of the text. If an editor warns you that the revised manuscript will be treated as a new submission, he or she is hinting that major revisions are needed. And when the door is closed, the editor never wants to see your manuscript again in any form or language. Don't antagonize the editor by resubmitting a revised draft as a new manuscript or sending a whiny letter of protest, which is the researcher version of entitled grade-grubbing. It's more dignified to take some lumps, rework the paper, and send it somewhere else.

The word *reject* in a decision letter doesn't necessarily mean that you can't resubmit the manuscript. Many editors use *reject* to refer to any manuscript that they aren't accepting outright: They're "rejecting" your first draft but expect to accept the revised one. In such cases, the journal's online portal is usually easier to interpret because it classifies a decision into practical categories, like "Accept With Minor Revisions" or "Major Revision." If the door is open for resubmission, you should almost always revise and resubmit. You have cheated the gods of rejection rates, so collect some burnt offerings, do a happy dance, and then revise your paper as quickly as possible. It is rarely rational to send your paper elsewhere instead of resubmitting it, but it might be if the journal wants changes that you're unwilling or unable to make. But beware the temptation to submit elsewhere when faced with a daunting revision. It's a subtle way of avoiding the tedious labor of revising.

After you commit to revise and resubmit your manuscript, you need to make a plan. Examine the editor's letter and the reviews and extract the *action points*—the targets for change. Many reviews are discursive and meandering; a long review might have only a few action points. Underline each comment that implies a change—adding something, rewording something, amputating something. After you identify the action points, revise the manuscript quickly. Your paper is close to publication, so don't slow down now (see Chapter 3).

For each action point, you have three options. First, you can make the change. Editors and reviewers have a lot of good ideas, so embrace change. Nothing puts you in the dramatic-and-erratic category like refusing to make simple changes, such as combining tables, deleting a figure, or reducing the word count by 10%. If you have an itchy urge to lash out at strangers who disagree with you on obscure and trivial matters, perhaps there's an Internet nearby where you can get it out of your system. Second, you can resist a suggestion. Along with their many good ideas, editors and reviewers have some that seem ill-considered, uninformed, or unproductive. If you don't make a suggested change, your revision letter will need to spend some time explaining your reasons. And third, you can punt the decision back to the editor. You'll occasionally see a suggestion that is probably unimportant but you're not sure how to handle it, such as when reviewers suggest changing your title, chopping the paper in half, or adding a bunch of figures for peripheral findings. In such cases, it's fine to punt the issue to the editor: "To save space and keep the paper focused, we decided not to add the four new figures suggested by Reviewer 2, but we could if you think it would improve the paper."

When you resubmit your manuscript, you'll need to send a cover letter that describes how you handled the criticisms and comments. Here is where the publishing game is won or lost. Editors are busy, harried people who have a backlog of decision letters to write and plenty of good manuscripts to pick from. Like the rest of us, they appreciate a quick win. If you send them a reasonable, comprehensive, and low-drama cover letter, they can get a quick win by accepting your manuscript and moving on to the next one in their pile. But many letters are dramatic and erratic, seething with indignation and wounded pride, and others read like postcards from a dreary vacation ("thanks for your comments—here's our revised manuscript").

Here's what a good revision letter looks like:

- Create headings, organized by reviewer, for each set of action points. Make a set of headings—start with *Editor's Comments* followed by *Reviewer 1's Comments*, *Reviewer 2's Comments*, and so on. Within each heading, address each action point in the order in which it was raised in the reviews. Numbered lists are easier for editors than a discursive, essay-style letter, so keep it crisp and clipped.
- Tackle each action point with a three-part system: (a) briefly summarize the comment or criticism; (b) describe what you did in response to this comment, if anything, and cite page or line numbers in the revised manuscript when possible; and

(c) discuss how your changes resolve the comment. When several reviewers raise the same action point—contrary to beginners' complaints, reviewers usually agree—you should mention the issue again each time it is raised. Simply dispatch it by noting the comment and referring to the number of your earlier discussion.

- Don't be fawning and obsequious. Editors don't expect you to refer to the reviewers' comments as masterful, wonderful, or insightful. You'll sound gratingly ingratiating.

And what do we do after submitting our revision letter and revised manuscript back to the journal? We turn to the next paper in the backlog, naturally.

Frequently Grumbled Grumblings About Journals

"They're Just Going to Reject My Paper"

Many writers get paralyzed by their fear of criticism and rejection. They'll put off finishing their manuscript because they're nervous about what happens after it leaves the nest and enters the cold, hard world of peer review. They imagine one reviewer scowling, another reviewer grimacing, and an editor slowly shaking her head as she fumbles for her enormous red *REJECT* stamp. And it is a hard world out there. Manuscripts, like sea turtle hatchlings, face many hazards during their harrowing journey from the nest to the open sea, and many never make it.

But rejection is a fact of academic life that we must accept. Most journals reject most of the papers they receive, so expecting rejection is rational. If a journal rejects 80% of its submissions, then its base rate of acceptance is 20%. Without any other information, 20% is the only rational estimate of our paper's chance of getting accepted. Because good journals rarely have acceptance rates above 50%, we should marvel at how many people get published, not despair at the inevitability of rejection.

"That's bleak," some might say. "How can you be motivated to write if you expect rejection?" I suppose we all write manuscripts for the same reason baby sea turtles scrabble toward the sea. Writing is a species-typical behavior for academics, much like reading old books and voting in local elections. We feel an urge to share our ideas, but these ideas must go through the harrowing journey of peer review. This process is imperfect—a few sickly sea turtles make it to sea, and a few hardy ones get picked off by seabirds—but in the long run peer review sharpens our ideas and strengthens our field.

"I Can't Fit Everything in"

Journal articles are small vessels for our ideas, so beginning writers get stuck when they can't cram all their thoughts into their article. "I can't fit it all in," they say. "The manuscript gets too long when I say everything I want to say." This is a good problem to have, I suppose, because it means you have a lot to say. If a research topic is worth studying, a short journal article shouldn't exhaust our ideas. Some of the mental surplus can be used as the seeds for other articles or for talks, book chapters, and essays. You might have a thesis that needs a book-sized vessel (see Chapter 7).

But most of our excess ideas are drab and dreary: arcane implications that few readers will care to hear; long explications of secondary, tertiary, and quaternary findings; and lengthy reviews of the literature that your thesis committee wanted to see but your readers already know. People are more likely to read and understand articles that are focused and compact— that make a few important points well—so most of the secondary ideas should be chopped. Hacking down the brush and brambles of peripheral ideas can feel wrenching, but your readers will see farther when they're gone.

"They're Going to Make Me Change Everything"

Some writers struggle to finish a paper because they believe that all their hard work will be undone by meddlesome reviewers. "Why bother making it great," they think, "when they're just going to make me change everything anyway?" My peevish and stubborn side resonates with this "You're not the boss of me!" outlook, but it isn't true. Editing a journal isn't like restoring a vintage car, where you strip it down to the metal frame and rebuild it with new parts. Instead, editors just scrap your jalopy of a paper and select a new, shiny one that won't embarrass the neighbors. Editors get more good papers than they have space for, so they'll reject your paper if it needs overhauling.

We must be willing to make big changes to our papers. Science holds published research to high standards and uses peer review to provide quality control. Our scholarly journals are our public and permanent record. Your article will be printed on acid-free paper and archived on library shelves for eternity, however long that is these days. Progress is faster when people connect their work to others' ideas, apply methods that meet modern standards, and confront awkward questions about their research. Journals are not the place for us to pitch wild ideas, dump malformed projects, and uncork opinionated rants. Fortunately, the Internet invented blogs and social media for us to do all that.

So, yes, we will be asked to change our papers, and sometimes those changes will be extensive. And in virtually every case, those changes make our papers better.

CONCLUSION

When struggling to write their first article, some writers lament, "Why would they care about my research?" If *they* refers to the world at large, they probably won't track down and read your article. But if *they* refers to researchers in your subfield, then you should expect some interest in your article. Your paper might be rejected once or twice before it finds a home, but a good paper will always find a good home. To write good articles, pick your journal first, outline according to the standard templates, submit great first drafts, and craft excellent resubmission letters.

After you have published a few articles, you'll find that the world of peer-reviewed journals isn't scary, merely slow. And after mastering the articles game, you might be ready for a bigger challenge—writing a book.

7

Writing Books

People engage in many curious practices. Whether we're reading essays on the Internet about how to spend less time online or watching nature documentaries in climate-controlled rooms, we humans have earned our reputation as nature's quirkiest mammals. Writing scholarly books, this chapter's curious practice, isn't as odd as chopping down a fir tree, dragging it into one's living room, and asking small children to hang fragile trinkets from its branches, but the more books I write, the more peculiar it seems.

This chapter is for people who are new to book writing. Some of you are wading through your first book, hip-deep and far from shore; others are watching from dry land, tempted to dive into writing but unsure of what the water is like. We'll discuss the motivational and practical aspects of writing books that newcomers ought to know. This chapter focuses on scholarly books, the sort written for fellow scholars, students, or practitioners and usually published by academic publishers. We won't delve into textbooks or mass-market books for general audiences because those rarely are (and probably shouldn't be) your first crack at writing a book.

You may be tempted to skip this chapter, thinking "No way—I'll *never* write a book." But you're probably doing a lot of things you never thought you'd do, like taking up jogging, avoiding gluten, or breeding Alsatians, so we capricious humans should never say never.

WHY WRITE A BOOK?

Why do people write academic books? In some fields of scholarship, writing books is simply what they do. For scholars in "book fields" like history, classics, religious studies, and literary criticism, books are the coin of their intellectual realms. Getting hired, tenured, and promoted requires coming up with appealing ideas, developing those ideas into big manuscripts, and persuading one of a shrinking number of scholarly publishers to publish it as a book. In the humanities, books are both noble career landmarks and greasy tools for staving off unemployment.

Outside the book fields, motives for writing books are murkier. In some departments, such as sociology or anthropology, you'll find both book writers (e.g., social theorists) and article writers (e.g., quantitative number crunchers). In some of the sciences, where the grants are big and the articles are short, few people even consider the possibility of writing a book.

Exhibit 7.1 describes the most common reasons for writing books. Have a look and see if any of them resonate with you. A few reasons might seem surprising (e.g., discovering that you've been inadvertently writing a book) and others might seem scary (e.g., writing a book to learn a new field), but they're all common ones. You don't need a pure or noble reason to write a book, but you should think seriously about why you want to write one before committing to it. Writing books hurts like no other kind of writing. Unlike the acute pain of grant writing, which goes away once the deadline passes, the chronic aches and fevers of book writing will afflict you for years.

EXHIBIT 7.1. Why Do We Write Scholarly Books?

- *Because we want to make a difference in the real world.* Practitioners—clinicians, educators, policymakers, and other people in the trenches—buy and read our books but rarely read our articles. Even if they could coax our articles from behind their paywalls, practitioners would rather read the big-picture, integrated view that a book provides.
- *Because our ideas are huge.* As any philologist or medievalist will tell you, some ideas require a book-sized box. In non-book fields, people write books to integrate evidence across many disciplines, introduce readers to a complicated topic, or serve as a final statement on a long line of research.

(continues)

EXHIBIT 7.1. Why Do We Write Scholarly Books? *(continued)*

■ *Because we want to learn something new.* In the writing to learn model (Zinsser, 1988), writing is a way of teaching ourselves what we know. If you want to learn a new area of scholarship, committing to write something about it forces you to read widely, critically, and thoughtfully. And after doing all that reading, you will surely have something worth writing about.

■ *Because we were inadvertently writing one.* Just as people can give birth without knowing they were pregnant, scholars can write a big book without knowing it. This often happens with course materials. An instructor who is unhappy with the textbook will write some supplementary essays, add another one the next semester, and eventually end up with 90% of a textbook.

■ *Because we want to plant a flag.* If you're interested in public scholarship, a book plants a flag: It signals your expertise to journalists, policymakers, and community groups who might seek it (Stein & Daniels, 2017). Likewise, if you want to do consulting or public speaking, publishing a book on the topic attracts the attention of clients and audiences.

■ *Because we're intellectually restless.* Some people are occasionally afflicted with intellectual wanderlust—the vague feeling that life would be better if they had a vast obligation looming over them for the next few years.

■ *Because we wandered into the wrong side of campus.* More than a few scientists have been infected with the urge to write a book after spending time with the philologists and medieval historians, hardened desperadoes known for their corrupting influence.

■ *Because books are amazing.* I've never heard someone say, "I just love downloaded modules," "I really should spend less time reading real books and more time online," or "I'm looking forward to having kids so we can cuddle up and read information and content together." Only books are books—cherished, respected, beloved.

Planning Your Book

If you're thinking about writing a book, the first step is to keep thinking about it. There's no rush—books will still exist when you're ready, and the hardest part of writing a book is figuring out what it's about. Unlike articles, books have a huge scope and scale. They have a thesis that gets developed across many chapters, a framework for organizing the freakish amount of information, and an audience that the book must reach and convince to be a success. Not surprisingly, writers have written books about writing books, so you can start your planning by reading. For scholarly books, I particularly recommend *Getting It Published* (Germano, 2016) and *Developmental Editing* (Norton, 2009).

You have to solve three planning problems. First, who is your book for? Who do you expect to buy and read it? Notice that we aren't asking who will notice it, who will find the idea interesting, or who will be glad to hear that someone wrote a book on that topic. Your book can't be all things to all audiences. It's better to serve a small, core audience well than to write a diffuse, generic book that no group in particular finds relevant or satisfying.

Second, what's the point of your book? What is it arguing? When they close the book, what will your readers believe or know? What, in short, is your thesis? Your thesis isn't simply your topic or concept. It's the point you want to make, the argument you want to develop, that serves as the organizing force for your book. As Norton (2009) put it, "A thesis can beguile, inspire, enrage—whatever works to grab the readers' attention. . . . A thesis is a gauntlet thrown down before readers, daring them to think back" (p. 48). To lure readers through your book, you need an appealing and intriguing thesis that can be captured in a couple sentences.

And third, what is your book's skeleton? What are the book's parts, and how are they arranged? What's the length, scale, and scope? Take your time: These early choices will dictate many seasons of research and writing. Once you have mapped the size and scope of your book, you'll see fissures in your ideas that suggest distinct chapters. And once you have a set of chapters, each of roughly equal length, and outlines for each chapter, you'll have a table of contents—the book writer's version of seeing the baby on the ultrasound monitor.

CONSIDER COAUTHORS

In some fields, all books have only one author. The abstemious humanities, for example, have an entrenched cultural taboo against coauthored books. I wouldn't want you to be stigmatized and driven from your department in a hail of reusable water bottles and sensible shoes, so conform to your local culture if it discourages coauthorship. But in more profligate fields, it's common to see two or three authors band together for a book. If coauthorship is an option, should you consider it?

If you haven't written a book before, teaming up with an experienced book author makes sense. The "mentor model" of coauthorship, common in the social sciences, pairs a grizzled book-writing veteran with a junior colleague. Their goal is not simply to write a book together, but for one person to teach another how to do it. Two productive writers with good writing habits and charitable and forgiving temperaments can write well together. It won't be much faster than writing alone, but it will give camaraderie to the lonesome task and polyphony to the book's ideas.

Binge writers, having some inchoate self-awareness about their writing struggles, love the idea of having a coauthor, so they'll latch on to anyone with strong writing habits. Be wary. If someone wants to write a book with you, ask if he or she has the writing habits that could yield one good manuscript page a week, every week, every month, be it in the summer or semester, every season, until you are both a few years older. Mentoring a new writer in the craft of books isn't the same as carrying someone. And when two binge writers decide to write a book together, needless to say, they risk a disaster of the sort described in ancient epigraphs.

WRITING THE THING

Writing a book is like writing anything else: a gallimaufry of reading, thinking, typing, and complaining, speckled with sparkles of intellectual delight. But books, with their menagerie of arguments, are much more complex than articles, which usually house only one pet idea. These different scopes and scales lure writers into an irrational *like-goes-with-like* style of thinking: "Sure, short articles can be written in short blocks of time during the week, but a big book requires a big block. I need a sabbatical."

You don't need a sabbatical. If you wait two years for a sabbatical and then write your manuscript in 6 months, did you write your book in 6 months or 30 months? Waiting for a sabbatical to work on a book is the same old "Big Blocks of Time" specious barrier (see Chapter 2) magnified from "I should stay home all day Friday to write" to "I need to go into hiding in rural Alsace for a year." Indeed, if anything, we should avoid what Wymann (2016) called "the horror of the sabbatical" (p. 28), the cycle of false hope, dashed expectations, and bitter regret that book writers usually experience.

But you do need to prune your obligations when you're writing a book during the normal work week. Few people will have the luxury of writing only their book, forswearing all other projects, but all of us can set wiser priorities. Your writing time is precious, so some kinds of writing are no longer worth your time when you're writing a book. You should decline marginal writing projects, such as invitations to write entries for scholarly encyclopedias and dictionaries, book reviews, newsletter essays, guest blog posts, and other book brambles. And think carefully before agreeing to write chapters for edited books—feed your own book before feeding someone else's.

You'll need to find a way for your short-term writing projects to coexist with your book. One strategy is to divide your weekly writing time. If you write every weekday, for example, you might devote Monday and Tuesday to articles and the other days to your book. If that seems too Solomonic, another approach is to pause the book occasionally, such as when a revise-and-resubmit decision for an article arrives, and then resume the book. Avoid pausing the book for more than a month, lest it go into hibernation for a whole season.

Your book is made up of an unbearably large number of paragraphs sorted into sections that are sorted into chapters. It's tempting to skip from chapter to chapter, working on the fun paragraphs and easy sections, but the chapter is the basic unit of your book. An author flitting between the pieces of low-hanging fruit could write a hundred pages without completing a chapter, so finish one chapter before moving to the next one. Many authors start with the second chapter and plow ahead in order; others write chapters out of order. However you do it, it is wise to save the introductory chapter and preface for last. Books usually wriggle away from their authors, maturing and evolving, so you should wait to see what you wrote before saying what you'll write.

FINDING A PUBLISHER

Authors write manuscripts for publishers to turn into books for readers to buy. It's easier to find a publisher in some fields than others. Each field has a ratio of its authors' supply of manuscripts and its readers' demand for books. In most of the humanities, the ratio is grim. The audience is small but every scholar wants to (or has to) write a book, so editors can be picky and fickle. Germano (2016) offered wise advice about how to find, approach, and work with publishers that writers in the humanities should take to heart.

But in other scholarly fields—humanities scholars should probably avert their eyes—supply and demand are flipped. Fields like psychology and biology, for example, have enormous audiences but relatively few authors. Because the market is huge but no one wants to write books, many editors are fishing in the same small pond of authors.

When it's time to find a publisher, start with your informal networks. Ask your book-writing colleagues about a good home for your project and any juicy gossip about publishers that they can dish. Then browse your shelves. Who releases books that you read and admire? Who published the books that your book talks about? Beginners often fear that publishers won't want a manuscript that's similar to their recent releases. To the contrary, publishers can't be all things to all readers, so they seek to build reputations for excellence in some areas. While there is surely a point at which your book overlaps too much with another, publishers are more likely to want to see your manuscript if it would slot nicely into an ongoing book series or area of excellence.

You're ready to talk to an editor about your book when you have a clear concept, a tight thesis, and a solid table of contents. The best place to cross paths with editors are at conferences, where publishers show their wares. Some of the nicely dressed people surrounded by tables and shelves of books work in sales and marketing, hoping to sell copies and encourage course adoptions. Others are acquisitions editors. They spend the conference meeting with prospective authors like you, attending sessions to see what topics are hot, and tracking down authors with long overdue manuscripts like flinty-eyed bounty hunters. Editors book much of their conference time early, so it's worth getting in touch via email to briefly describe your project and ask if you could meet at the conference to discuss it. But there's nothing wrong with a cold call. You can always wander up to a table early in the conference and ask if someone from acquisitions is there.

If intrigued by your book, editors will encourage you to send them a book proposal. You'll get proposal guidelines from the publisher, but you should read up on book proposals (Germano, 2016) and ask your friends in the department for advice and feedback before submitting it. The typical proposal asks the author to describe the book's thesis, intended audience, and major competitors. You'll need a detailed table of contents, usually with several paragraphs that describe each chapter, along with sample chapters.

The publishers will want to know a lot about you, too, to see if you're a credible and marketable messenger for the idea.

Unlike journal articles, book proposals can be submitted simultaneously to several publishers, but it isn't always worth doing so. You should inform publishers that you're shopping the proposal around and let them know if another publisher offers a contract. But if you have a clear favorite, you might send your proposal only to that publisher and note that you aren't sending it elsewhere. The world of scholarly publishing is small, and good manners will help you develop long-term relationships with publishers.

After the proposal is perused by peer reviewers, the editor may offer you a contract—another milestone for a book. Contracts specify a great many things, but the most important for us here are the *length* and the *delivery date*. The manuscript that you deliver to the publisher should roughly be what you promised. If it's too long or too short, or if it has many more figures, maps, and illustrations than promised, the book might fall outside the range of what the publisher can effectively print and market.

And your manuscript must be delivered on time. You and the publisher will negotiate a delivery date, and you better meet that date. Faculty grouse about students turning in work late, but professorial tardiness is legion in publishing. Academic authors so rarely deliver their manuscripts on time—one imagines that unrealistic optimism, binge writing, and waiting for sabbaticals have something to do with it—that your publisher will be surprised and impressed.

Dealing With the Details

Your manuscript's end will be anticlimactic. When that last paragraph is written, the clouds won't part and fireworks won't go off. Instead, you'll face a pile of humdrum tasks: gathering permissions forms, making high-quality electronic figures and illustrations, and tracking down obscure sources. The publisher probably has an extensive author questionnaire for you that asks for information about you and about your book that they use for cataloging, marketing, and promotion. You may be asked to suggest cover art and scholars who might provide blurbs for the cover.

When your book enters production, you might get a copyedited manuscript—an edited manuscript to review before it is typeset—and you will surely get page proofs. These page proofs are urgent. Your perfectionist academic mind will realize that this is your last chance to tinker and fiddle with the text, but the publisher needs those back quickly and with only minor corrections. It's worth asking (or hiring) a keen-eyed friend to scour the proofs, just in case the typo imps changed *assess* to *asses* again. Your book gets indexed at the proofs stage. Some publishers will index the book for you; others will ask you to do it or give you the option, should your heart be inclined toward indexing's dark allure. And eventually a box full of books arrives, your bubble-wrapped bundle of joy.

Thinking About the Next Book

Even if you swore you would write only one book, even if writing that book harmed your relationship with your pets and with caffeine in equal measure, you'll think about writing another one. You will. Once you hold the bound book in your hands and your memory of writing it becomes gauzy and sepia-toned, you'll think that your book might want a sibling to hang out with on the shelf. And people will surely pester you about your plans. Acquisitions editors will notice your first book and get in touch. If you work in a book-writing field, your friends in the department will display an unseemly and lurid curiosity about your next project.

Writing the second book is much easier and much harder than the first. You'll have the confidence that comes from having done something hard, and you'll know more about how book writing works and what publishers want to see. But you'll also have bigger intellectual ambitions. Second books usually have a larger scope, a more daring thesis, or a wider audience, so they'll vex you in ways your first book didn't.

Your mind might drift to thinking of writing a textbook, the oddest creature in the book bestiary. The textbook market, for better or worse, isn't what it once was. Textbooks are huge risks for publishers and authors. If you're inclined to write a textbook because of daydreams of untold wealth, you would probably make more money regularly selling your plasma. A few textbooks make big money, but most textbooks fall flat and fail: the book is published, few instructors adopt it, the publisher declines to develop a second edition, and the loud *whoosh* of dreams deflating fills the halls. The best textbooks—books that are integrative, ambitious, and forward looking—are more likely to meet this ignominious end. Because these failed books vanish into history, aspiring textbook writers don't appreciate just how speculative textbook writing can be.

But whatever you choose to write, you now know how to write a book: weekly, according to a writing schedule.

CONCLUSION

Writing a book is like injecting anabolic steroids: If it doesn't kill you, it'll make you stronger and hairier. But I know you can do it. When your book is going slow and looking bleak, go to the campus library and gaze upon the rows and rows of books. Some of those authors were more stylish and diligent writers than you and me. But some of them were duller and flakier than us, and they finished their book. There is no mystery to book writing, only the ineluctable routine of following your writing schedule.

More people should consider writing a book, but books aren't for everyone. If while reading this chapter, for example, you thought "I'm way too busy with grants to write a book," you might be right, as our next chapter shows.

8

Writing Proposals for Grants and Fellowships

Adulthood is not nearly as glamorous as I thought it would be when I was a kid. I had planned on wearing X-ray glasses while driving my flying car; now I'd be happy finding my cheap sunglasses in the maelstrom of my minivan. "Fight the power!" evolved into "Because I said so." But for some things, all the old advice works. Haste does make waste, one vice can indeed support two children, and there are millions of other fish in the industrial aquaculture facility.

It pains me when this happens—my professor side would like everything to be counterintuitive and complex—but sometimes we should admit that common sense is both common and sensible for a reason. In this chapter, we delve into the common sense of proposals for grants and fellowships. Our discussion applies to all kinds of proposals—from huge federal research grants in the sciences to small travel-grants and fellowships in the humanities—because the principles of successful proposals are mostly the same.

MOST GRANT WRITING CLICHÉS ARE TRUE

So you want to write your first grant proposal—what should you do? Exhibit 8.1 lists the standard things you always hear. If you go to a grant-writing workshop, browse online, or pester an old-timer for advice, you'll hear all these tips, always, from everyone. Take a minute to read through it. If you're like most academics, you'll have a twinge of ambivalence. That part of your mind that survived years of graduate training—the small voice of conventional wisdom that likes classic rock and suspects that doughnuts can't be as unhealthy as "they" say—will read the list and think, "Sure, sounds obvious. That all makes a lot of sense. I'll do it."

But that other part of your mind—the one honed and sharpened by graduate school, the one that prefers discourse to talking, text to writing, pedagogy to teaching—will think, "That's the same old stuff everyone says. There must be more to it than that." I hear you and acknowledge your suspicion of popular wisdom. After writing Exhibit 8.1, I felt an unsettling urge to buy pleated khakis and a knit polo shirt. The vaunted "wisdom of the crowd" is nearly always folly, but not when it comes to grant writing. I wouldn't jump off a bridge just because everyone else at work was doing it, but I might if they all had lots of grants and assured me that it would improve my proposals.

EXHIBIT 8.1. Conventional Wisdom for Grant-Writing

- Your institution has an office that manages grants and submits proposals on your behalf. Contact this office as soon as you start thinking seriously about submitting something. Meet with them to learn what they will need from you and what they can do for you.

- Plan to wrap up your proposal at least 2 weeks before it is due—the earlier, the better. This gives your institution time to route and process everything. (So few people do this that the grants staff will notice and appreciate your diligence. Someday you might be a bit late or need an urgent favor, and they will remember.)

- Read the funding agency's call for proposals—every last word, no matter how boring.

- Read the funding agency's submission guidelines and instructions—every last word, no matter how boring.

- If the funding agency holds a workshop or webinar you can attend, attend it. If they have posted videos on their submission and review process, watch them.

- When possible, discuss your idea with someone at the funding agency, such as a program official or grants coordinator.

- Get examples of recent funded and unfunded proposals. If you don't know who to ask, your institution's grants office can usually get some samples for you.

- Ask someone to give you feedback on a draft of your proposal. This person might be local (e.g., someone in your department who has had good fortune) or off-site (e.g., someone your institution pays to provide a mock peer review).

FOOD FOR FUNDED THOUGHT

If it helps you join the herd and get with the program, consider Exhibit 8.1 as "the syllabus" for grant-writing—it covers the basics that you should follow to get a good grade. But what else can you do to make the muses of external funding smile favorably upon your humble efforts? Here are some ideas that should improve your odds over the long run.

DON'T WRITE A GRANT—WRITE GRANTS

Some things in life should not be done only once. I will leave most of them up to your overactive imagination, but writing grant proposals is one such thing. Writing your first grant is like teaching your very first class—there's so much more to it than you thought. But your second time teaching that class is much easier, and the third is easier still. And most of that knowledge transfers when you create a new class—you already know the nuts-and-bolts of making a syllabus, creating lectures and assessments, and chanting the levels of Bloom's taxonomy with your robes and thurible.

It isn't worth learning how to plan, write, and submit grant proposals if you intend to submit only one. Your first complex federal proposal, like a National Institutes of Health research grant or a National Endowment for the Humanities fellowship, will hurt. No one has forms, instructions, and guidelines like the feds do. But the second proposal is much easier, and the third is easier still. From the beginning, then, you need a "grants, not a grant" mind-set. The decision, for example, is not "Should I write an NEH fellowship?" but "Should I submit an NEH fellowship proposal at least every few years until I get one?" It's better to invest in books and articles than to dabble with grant proposals.

ARE YOU AN ELEPHANT OR A SEAHORSE?

Some creatures, like elephants, give birth to relatively few babies but invest heavily in them. Other creatures, like seahorses, give birth to thousands of babies but invest little in them. What's your grant-writing species? Some scholars are grant elephants. Because they slowly gestate their proposals, they don't submit many of them, but their proposals are always ready for the world. Other scholars are grant seahorses. Because they churn out proposals, they're not emotionally attached to any single one and know that most of them will be eaten by the crustaceans on the review panel.

Elephants submit to only a few sponsors. A pachydermatic psychologist who studies depression, for example, might submit only to the National Institutes of Health and to a private foundation devoted to mental health. Over time, elephants develop tacit knowledge, expertise, and relationships with the sponsors that increase the odds that their fledgling proposals will be viable. Seahorses, in contrast, submit to a huge set of sponsors. Federal agencies, large charities, small foundations, local nonprofits, random passersby with change jingling loudly in their pockets—they'll all get proposals.

Although I'm more *Elephantidae* than *Hippocampinae*, no one species is right for everyone. An elephant seeks success through strategy and craft; its natural habitat is a college or university department that values grants but doesn't require external funding for promotion. A seahorse seeks success through volume and probability; its natural habitat is wherever soft-money jobs are found, such as medical schools, think tanks, and free-standing research centers. The middle ground—giving too little attention to too few proposals—isn't evolutionarily stable, so you should pick a side.

COMPETE ON YOUR HOME FIELD

No matter how humble your field of scholarship might be, it's yours. Your home field—your primary scholarly topic—is where you have the highest profile and the strongest reputation. When you write grant proposals, you want to compete on your home field. Getting grants is hard enough without having to grind out a victory in someone's else stadium. Nevertheless, researchers chasing money often find themselves far from home. They see a funding opportunity announcement for some hot topic and think, "Hey, we might be able to come up with an idea for that."

Any field with funding has three groups of researchers competing for it. Imagine, for example, that a funding opportunity announcement comes out on a pressing biomedical topic, perhaps the early detection of dementia. Three groups of scientists will apply.

The first and smallest group has the researchers who fundamentally study that topic—they're playing on their home field—and some of them are the field's most important and influential scholars. Dementia research is what they do: they've been studying it for a while, and all the best grad students and postdocs want to work with them. This group will get most of the grants.

The second group has the researchers whose work has something to offer the problem. They don't fundamentally study dementia, in our example, but their work overlaps with the problem and can credibly inform it. This group will get some funding, but not as much. The third, and largest, group has the broad community of researchers who do work that tangentially touches the field. They could—with some stretching and spinning—look like credible players, but they fundamentally study something else. Their proposals rarely stick.

Don't be that third group that chases money. Grant proposals are funded relatively ("Is this one of the best proposals that we received this round?") rather than absolutely ("Is this proposal good?"). It doesn't matter if your proposal is good, or even great, in its own right—it must be better than most of the other proposals, and nearly all of them are pretty good. And once you realize that the best-known researchers in a field are always applying, you see why you need to compete on your home field. When an intriguing funding opportunity announcement comes out, don't think,

"I bet we can form an appealing team and try to get in on that." Instead, before applying, we should ask ourselves, "many of the most famous scholars in that field are going to apply, too. Can we, as interlopers, beat them on their home field?"

BRIDESMAIDS HAVE MORE FUN

In the humanities, a grant or fellowship usually has only one applicant—the person visiting the archive, writing the book, or interrogating the textual materiality. In the sciences, however, a grant proposal usually has a big, cheery team, much like a wedding party. Its bride is the Principal Investigator (PI), the person responsible for executing and managing the project; its bridesmaids go by many names—Co-Investigators, Collaborators, Consultants, or Coattail Riders, depending on what they do. They support the PI by bringing focused skills, such as recruiting a hard-to-reach sample, applying a tool or method, or making centerpieces from mason jars and mulberry twigs.

The PI has the most glamorous role, but everyone knows that the bridesmaids have more fun. Indeed, you can get married only so many times. Grant mavens are rarely the PI on all, or even most, of their funded projects. Instead, they're plugged into several teams where they can attract some funding for their work and contribute to an interesting project. If your home field isn't especially fertile for funding, you can cultivate skills that make you an effective collaborator. People with

122

expertise in complicated, technical topics—especially methodological and statistical expertise—who can write quickly will attract more offers to collaborate on proposals than they can handle.

DON'T DESPAIR

Some areas of scholarship are barren deserts for grant funding. Scholars in the humanities might submit 20 fellowship proposals in the hopes of getting $8,000 to visit a distant archive or writing retreat. Scholars in the life sciences, in contrast, can request a few million dollars from NIH—a small slice of the tens of billions it awards each year—with a relatively short proposal. It is what it is. The world isn't fair. If you're in the humanities, the grass really is much greener on the other side, largely because of their big budget for fertilizer and landscaping.

If you work in a funding desert, don't despair. It isn't an indictment of the value of your research field. Exhibit 8.2 provides a slightly cynical list of factors that predict whether an area of research will be flush with funding. But what can you do about it? One option is to change your area of scholarship. Many desert-dwellers pack up and move to more fertile fields. Some researchers retool to learn new methods and skills, others develop a secondary line of work with more funding potential, and a few shift their interests entirely to whatever is hot and profitable. I'm not necessarily advocating for this option, but it makes sense for some scholars. For most

EXHIBIT 8.2. The Geography of Grant Deserts

When viewed cynically, the world of grants is oddly rational. You can predict how much funding a research area gets with a few factors.

- *Does the topic appeal to politicians?* Federal agencies are the big players in scholarly funding. A handful of motivated politicians can create new agencies with multimillion dollar budgets, such as when a few influential senators interested in bee pollen and cow colostrum sparked the creation of the National Center for Complementary and Alternative Medicine (Atwood, 2003).
- *Does the topic appeal to people who show up to vote?* Many medical researchers suspect that it isn't a coincidence that funding for diseases of aging vastly outstrips funding for diseases of childhood.
- *Is the topic politically stigmatized?* If you're an American studying topics like climate change, the failure of abstinence-based approaches to sexual education, and the sunny sides of prohibited drugs, you know what I mean.
- *Does the topic appeal to wealthy philanthropists?* A single wealthy patron with quirky interests can fund an entire area of scholarship.
- *Does the topic make powerful interests uncomfortable?* Critical and controversial approaches to fraught topics, such as gender, race, and education, get less funding than research projects that don't rock the yacht.
- *Does the topic make or save someone money or solve a pressing practical problem?* Corporate contracts are a huge source of funding if you have an idea that can make or save them money.

of us, though, we didn't get into academics to cater to the fickle priorities of funding agencies.

Another option is to decide not to bother with applying for grants. Instead of moving from your funding desert, you can grow where you're planted. Of course, you'll grow into a Bonker hedgehog cactus instead of a tropical cinnamon fern, but there's nothing wrong with that—the prickly spines might even keep a few pesky service assignments away. If your field's opportunities for funding are sparse, and if you can flourish in your job without funding, then forswearing the hassle of grants can be a thoughtful, rational choice. Time spent researching, writing, and submitting grants is time not spent writing the articles and books you're passionate about.

I think the sciences and humanities could use an intergroup empathy intervention (Stephan & Finlay, 1999). Some humanities scholars, cursing bitterly over the cornucopia of funding in the sciences, suspect that the chemistry faculty are lighting the Bunsen burners with $100 bills. In truth, funding supply and researcher supply always reach a depressing equilibrium. Any area of research with a lot of funding (e.g., diseases of aging) quickly attracts gaggles of young researchers, so the success rates collapse after a couple years. Nevertheless, researchers in funding-rich fields often must obtain grants to get promoted and tenured. In some medical science departments, for example, you'll be fired if you don't bring in 50%, 100%, or even 150% of your annual salary in funding each year, averaged over the past few years. The pressure can be crippling: If your next proposal doesn't get funded, you and everyone who works for you will be unemployed.

Likewise, the scientists think the humanities faculty have it easy. They don't have to apply for grants, and they won't get fired if they don't scrounge up funding from slow, opaque, and politicized federal agencies. And many scientists have keenly inquired why so many American scholars study problems in history and literature that require traveling to popular European tourist locations. Fair enough. But the scientists don't have to write long, complex books that require (a) reading dozens and dozens of other long, complex books, and (b) persuading one of a declining number of publishers to print it. In departments that require a book to be in-press for promotion and tenure, an assistant professor's career is at the mercy of how quickly book editors and external reviewers get around to the manuscript.

DON'T NEGLECT YOUR PUBLISHED WORK

All ecosystems have predators and prey. In our academic worlds, some of our goals and tasks are predators—they gobble other, weaker goals that didn't quite make it to shelter. Despite all our grousing at the end of the semester, teaching rarely gobbles writing. I genuinely believe, in a tacit way that's hard to articulate, that my writing and teaching are the same intellectual beast—much like a two-headed box turtle hatched in a fetid academic pond. Instead, writing gobbles writing. Some kinds of writing projects suck up time in your writing schedule with little payoff (see Silvia, 2015). In the marshy swampland of academic writing, your books and articles are fluffy, twee hatchlings, and your grant proposals are the invasive emerald tree boas that gobble them.

A good article manuscript will probably get published somewhere, and a good book manuscript will eventually find a publisher. But an unfunded grant proposal is dead in the water. Sometimes you can harvest a few pages for a manuscript, but when a grant proposal gets rejected you're usually left with a big carcass suitable only for taxidermy.

Juggling writing projects is endlessly vexing (see Chapter 3). Because unfunded grant proposals won't get published, they evaporate into history—along with the hours of writing time they gobbled that could have been spent on the sure-things of articles and books. Many scholars thus find themselves in a trap: They need grants for promotion and tenure, but they need publications, too. Time spent on articles and books usually pays off; time spent on grants, however, might be a boon but is usually a bust. When a department requires funding for promotion—common in the sciences—a writer could end up with no grants and few articles, the worst of both worlds.

This tension can't be resolved, but you can make your grant-writing more efficient by using some of the advice discussed earlier. In particular, focusing on only a couple sponsors, as elephants do, saves an enormous amount of time spent researching sponsors, learning their guidelines, and reworking your boilerplate materials. Likewise, focusing on your core expertise saves an enormous amount of time spent researching tangential fields of scholarship. Grant proposals will still compete with your articles and books, but they'll gobble less of your writing time if you're focused and strategic.

CONCLUSION

During a cathartic rant about grant writing, someone once told me, "I could write a book in the time it takes to write two grants." That sounds about right to me. A short psychology book might be around three or four big federal proposals; a book in history or religious studies might be seven or eight. Unless your job is to write grants, you shouldn't lose sight of why people apply for them. We have ideas we want to develop, projects we want to do, and things we want to say. Applying for grants can move those goals along, but we shouldn't let the allure of untold riches—and the resulting untold annual budget, compliance, and reporting forms that you hear less about—distract us from our books and articles.

9

"The Good Things Still to Be Written"

Graduate school is long enough for most grad students to eventually find themselves in need of towels. And so they drive their jalopy to the nearest big-box store, find the long row of towels, and stand in front of the cheapest ones—towels scratchy enough to refinish an oak table, towels unworthy of the name—with a practiced aspect of resignation and defeat. "One day," they say, looking with yearning at the fancy towels on the eye-level shelves, "when I have a real job, it will all be different."

Most of us made a solemn grad-school vow like this. Once the indentured servitude of grad school is over, things are going to change. I'll take a vacation, start a family, get a hobby, and buy my ramen noodles at hip fusion restaurants instead of dollar stores. But for now, I'll make some sacrifices so I can write all the stuff I need to write to get that job.

What happens after grad students get that coveted tenure-track job? They find themselves wading through the slowly rising waters of teaching and service, holding their writing projects over their heads to keep them safe and dry, and they think, "When I get tenure, it will all be different. I can slow down, take a vacation, start a family. But for now . . ."

And what happens once they get tenure? There's no secret ceremony. The provost won't walk up to you, put a hand on your shoulder, and say, "You're here now. It's time. Join us." Your department chair won't give you tokens for free hot-stone massages at a secret wellness spa concealed beneath the Faculty Center. Instead, your bosses will find many more service opportunities to suit someone of your obvious energy and talents— after all, you need to start planning for promotion to full professor. And so it goes, cycle to cycle, until we hear the late-career professors saying, "I can't wait to retire so I can finally focus on my book."

Let's commit to using the active voice instead of the passive "things will change" and "it is going to be different." I've been around long enough to know that it will not be different unless we choose to make it so. If we don't shoehorn our writing into the normal work week, no one will do it for us. We have all sacrificed too much in grad school to go back to binge writing and scratchy towels.

The Joys of Writing Schedules

Making a writing schedule and sticking to it—this book's central idea—strikes some people as dour and austere, but it has its joys. You'll write more pages per week, which translates into more journal articles, more grant proposals, and more books. Following a schedule eliminates the uncertainties and sorrows of "finding time to write," of wondering if something will get done. Projects will wrap up well before their deadlines. You'll spend as much time writing during the summer weeks, if you choose to write then, as you'll spend during the first weeks of the semester. Writing will become mundane, routine, and typical, not oppressive, uncertain, and monopolistic.

And writing schedules bring balance to your life and perspective on your writing. Binge writers search for big chunks of time, and they "find" this time during the evenings and weekends. Binge writing thus consumes time that should be spent on normal living. Our books, our articles, our ideas are important, without a doubt—but we are more than writers, so we should protect our real-world time just as we protect our scheduled writing time. Spend your leisure time hanging out, finding new trails, building canoes, agitating against The System, perfecting your apple fritter recipe, or holding a staring contest with your inscrutable cat. It doesn't matter what you do as long as you don't spend your free time writing—there's time during the work week for that.

Productive writing involves harnessing the power of habit, and habits come from repetition. Make a schedule and sit down to write during your scheduled time. You might spend the first few sessions groaning, gnashing your teeth, and draping yourself in sackcloth, but at least you're not binge gnashing. After a couple of weeks, once your writing schedule is habitual, you'll no longer feel pressured to write during nonscheduled hours. And a few months later, once your writing schedule has ossified into a weekly routine, the notion of "wanting to write" will seem irrelevant.

You don't need special traits, special genes, or special motivation to write a lot. And you don't need to want to write—people rarely feel like doing unpleasant tasks that lack deadlines—so don't wait until you feel like it. Make a writing schedule and show up for it. Want less and do more. "Decide what you want to do," wrote Zinsser (2006), "then decide to do it. Then do it" (p. 280).

Writing Isn't a Race

Write as much or as little as you want to write. Although this book shows you how to write a lot, don't think that you ought to. In a way, this book isn't about writing a lot: it's about slotting writing into your normal work week, which makes writing less stressful and lets you take the vacations that your grad-school self vowed that you would take. If you want to write more, a writing schedule will get you there. You'll spend more hours per week writing, write more efficiently, and chisel through your backlog. If you don't want to write more, a writing schedule will take the guilt and uncertainty out of writing. You won't worry about "finding time to write," and you won't sacrifice your weekends for writing binges. And if you plan to write only a few things in your career, your writing time can be time for thinking and reading about your professional development.

Publishing a lot does not make anyone a good person or scholar. Some of academia's most prolific writers rehash the same ideas ceaselessly: empirical articles lead to a review article, the review article gets rewarmed as book chapters, and the book chapters are retreaded for handbooks and newsletters. Prolific writers might have more publications, but they don't always have more good ideas than anyone else. Writing isn't a race. Don't count your publications unless you have to. Don't publish a paper just for the sake of having one more published paper, one more notch on the belt.

THE END

This book is over; thank you for reading it. I enjoyed writing this book, but it's time for me to write something else, and it's time for you to write something, too. Let's look forward to it. "When I think of the good things still to be written I am glad," wrote William Saroyan (1952), "for there is no end to them, and I know I myself shall write some of them" (p. 2).

References

Atkinson, J. W., & Birch, D. (1970). *The dynamics of action.* New York, NY: John Wiley & Sons.

Atwood, K. C. (2003). The ongoing problem with the National Center for Complementary and Alternative Medicine. *Skeptical Inquirer, 27*(5), 23–29.

Baker, S. (1969). *The practical stylist* (2nd ed.). New York, NY: Thomas Y. Crowell.

Bandura, A. (1997). *Self-efficacy: The exercise of control.* New York, NY: W.H. Freeman.

Boice, R. (1990). *Professors as writers: A self-help guide to productive writing.* Stillwater, OK: New Forums Press.

Carrier, J., Monk, T. H., Buysse, D. J., & Kupfer, D. J. (1997). Sleep and morningness–eveningness in the 'middle' years of life (20–59 y). *Journal of Sleep Research, 6,* 230–237. http://dx.doi.org/10.1111/j.1365-2869.1997.00230.x

Cirillo, F. (2018). *The Pomodoro Technique: The acclaimed time-management system that has transformed how we work.* New York, NY: Currency.

Fitzgerald, F. S. (1945). The crack-up. In E. Wilson (Ed.), *The crack-up* (pp. 69–84). New York, NY: New Directions.

Fitzgerald, F. S. (with Cowley, M.). (1955). *Tender is the night: A romance; with the author's final revision.* London, England: Penguin.

Fowler, A. (2006). *How to write.* Oxford, England: Oxford University Press.

Germano, W. (2016). *Getting it published: A guide for scholars and anyone else serious about serious books* (3rd ed.). Chicago, IL: University of Chicago Press. http://dx.doi.org/10.7208/chicago/9780226281544.001.0001

Gordon, K. E. (2003). *The new well-tempered sentence: A punctuation handbook for the innocent, the eager, and the doomed.* Boston, MA: Mariner Books.

Hale, C. (2013). *Sin and syntax: How to craft wickedly effective prose* (Rev. & updated ed.). New York, NY: Three Rivers Press.

Jellison, J. M. (1993). *Overcoming resistance: A practical guide to producing change in the workplace.* New York, NY: Simon & Schuster.

Kellogg, R. T. (1994). *The psychology of writing.* New York, NY: Oxford University Press.

Keyes, R. (2003). *The writer's book of hope: Getting from frustration to publication.* New York, NY: Holt.

King, S. (2000). *On writing: A memoir of the craft.* New York, NY: Scribner.

Kluckhohn, C., & Murray, H. A. (1948). Personality formation: The determinants. In C. Kluckhohn & H. A. Murray (Eds.), *Personality in nature, society and culture* (pp. 35–48). New York, NY: Knopf.

Korotitsch, W. J., & Nelson-Gray, R. O. (1999). An overview of self-monitoring research in assessment and treatment. *Psychological Assessment, 11,* 415–425. http://dx.doi.org/10.1037/1040-3590.11.4.415

Milstein, C. (2010). *Anarchism and its aspirations.* Oakland, CA: AK Press.

Nicolaus, M. (2014). *Empowering your sober self: The LifeRing approach to addiction recovery* (2nd ed.). Oakland, CA: LifeRing Press.

Norton, S. (2009). *Developmental editing: A handbook for freelancers, authors, and publishers.* Chicago, IL: Univer-

sity of Chicago Press. http://dx.doi.org/10.7208/chicago/
9780226595160.001.0001

Perry, S. K. (1999). *Writing in flow: Keys to enhanced creativity*.
Cincinnati, OH: Writer's Digest Books.

Pope-Hennessy, J. (1971). *Anthony Trollope*. London, England:
Phoenix Press.

Reis, H. T. (2000). Writing effectively about design. In R. J.
Sternberg (Ed.), *Guide to publishing in psychology journals*
(pp. 81–97). Cambridge, England: Cambridge University
Press. http://dx.doi.org/10.1017/CBO9780511807862.007

Salovey, P. (2000). Results that get results: Telling a good
story. In R. J. Sternberg (Ed.), *Guide to publishing in psychology journals* (pp. 121–132). Cambridge, England:
Cambridge University Press. http://dx.doi.org/10.1017/
CBO9780511807862.009

Saroyan, W. (1952). *A bicycle rider in Beverly Hills*. New York,
NY: Scribner.

Silvia, P. J. (2006). *Exploring the psychology of interest*.
New York, NY: Oxford University Press. http://dx.doi.org/
10.1093/acprof:oso/9780195158557.001.0001

Silvia, P. J. (2015). *Write it up: Practical strategies for writing
and publishing journal articles*. Washington, DC: American Psychological Association. http://dx.doi.org/10.1037/
14470-000

Smith, K. (2001). *Junk English*. New York, NY: Blast Books.

Stein, A., & Daniels, J. (2017). *Going public: A guide for social
scientists*. Chicago, IL: University of Chicago Press. http://
dx.doi.org/10.7208/chicago/9780226364810.001.0001

Stephan, W. G., & Finlay, K. (1999). The role of empathy in improving intergroup relations. *Journal of Social
Issues, 55*, 729–743. http://dx.doi.org/10.1111/0022-
4537.00144

Strunk, W., Jr., & White, E. B. (2000). *The elements of style*
(4th ed.). New York, NY: Longman.

Sword, H. (2017). *Air & light & time & space: How successful academics write*. Cambridge, MA: Harvard University Press.

Trollope, A. (1999). *An autobiography*. New York, NY: Oxford University Press. (Original work published 1883)

Wymann, C. (2016). *Mind your writing: Exploring academic writing*. Bern, Switzerland: Author.

Zinsser, W. (1988). *Writing to learn*. New York, NY: Harper & Row.

Zinsser, W. (2006). *On writing well: The classic guide to writing nonfiction* (7th ed.). New York, NY: Harper Perennial.

Index

About the Author

Paul J. Silvia, PhD, is the Lucy Spinks Keker Excellence Professor at the University of North Carolina at Greensboro. He received his doctorate in psychology from the University of Kansas in 2001. Among many other things, he studies the psychology of creativity and the arts, particularly how people come up with good ideas and why they find art interesting, appealing, and awe-inspiring. He received the Berlyne Award, an early-career award given by the Society for the Psychology of Aesthetics, Creativity, and the Arts, for his research on aesthetic emotions, and he later served as president of the Society. His other books include *Exploring the Psychology of Interest* (2006); *Public Speaking for Psychologists: A Lighthearted Guide to Research Presentations, Job Talks, and Other Opportunities to Embarrass Yourself* (2010, with David B. Feldman); and *Write It Up: Practical Strategies for Writing and Publishing Journal Articles* (2015). In his free time, Dr. Silvia restores vintage pocket watches, plays board and card games, and enjoys not writing.